BERNARD L. EINBOND

SAMUEL JOHNSON'S ALLEGORY

MOUTON

Once among the most highly regarded of Johnson's works, the allegorical essays and tales have been in the present century among the most neglected. Professor Einbond's book examines the entire body of Johnson's allegorical writings in the light of Johnson's critical pronouncements on the nature of allegory and the function of art. Through an understanding of Johnson's allegorical technique, the reader is enabled to come to a new critical appreciation of many of Johnson's most appealing works, including *Rasselas*, "The Vision of Theodore", and a number of the more interesting essays from *The Rambler* and *The Idler*.

Bernard Lionel Einbond is Assistant Professor of English at Herbert H. Lehman College (formerly Hunter College in The Bronx) of the City University of New York. He has also taught at Columbia College.

Born in New York City in 1937, he attended The Bronx High School of Science and Columbia College before beginning graduate study in English and Comparative Literature at Columbia University, where he received the Ph. D. degree in 1966. His own poetry has appeared in *American Haiku*, *Mutiny*, and other little magazines.

DE PROPRIETATIBUS LITTERARUM

edenda curat

C. H. VAN SCHOONEVELD

Indiana University

Series Practica, 24

SAMUEL JOHNSON'S ALLEGORY

by

BERNARD L. EINBOND

Herbert H. Lehman College
of the City University of New York

1971

MOUTON

THE HAGUE . PARIS

LIBRARY OF CONGRESS CATALOG CARD NUMBER: 76. 134541

Printed in Hungary

ACKNOWLEDGMENTS

I wish to express my gratitude to Professors James L. Clifford, Allen T. Hazen, and John Middendorf, three dedicated and devoted Johnsonian scholars, all of Columbia University, each of whom read the manuscript of this book in several of its stages and offered valuable criticism and needed encouragement. Among numerous colleagues and friends who provided various forms of assistance, I should like to name Thomas L. Canavan of Temple University, George Jochnowitz of Richmond College, and, at Lehman College, Richard J. Geehern, Leonard Lief, Victor B. Reed, and Edgar V. Roberts. In the final preparation of the manuscript for publication, I was aided by a faculty grant in support of research from Lehman College of the City University of New York.

Bronx, New York   BERNARD LIONEL EINBOND
January 1970

CONTENTS

Acknowledgments 5

Cue titles 8

Introduction 9

    I. Johnson and Poetic Form 13

    II. Allegory and Allegorical Metaphor 27

    III. Johnson on Allegory 34

    IV. The Allegorical Pun 45

    V. "The Vision of Theodore" 56

    VI. The *Rambler* Allegories 65

    VII. "Borderline Cases" 76

    VIII. *Rasselas:* The Happy Valley as Allegorical Metaphor   83

A Concluding Note 97

Selected Bibliography 99

Index 103

CUE TITLES

Works—*The Works of Samuel Johnson, LL. D.*, 11 vols. (Oxford, 1825).

Lives—*Lives of the English Poets by Samuel Johnson, LL. D.*, ed. George Birkbeck Hill, 3 vols (Oxford, Clarendon Press, 1905).

Idler and Adventurer—*The Yale Edition of the Works of Samuel Johnson,* Vol. II: *The Idler and The Adventurer*, ed. W. J. Bate, J. M. Bullitt, and L. F. Powell (New Haven, Yale University Press, 1963).

Dictionary—*A Dictionary of the English Language by Samuel Johnson, LL. D.*, 2 vols., 6th ed. (London, 1785).

Rasselas— Samuel Johnson, *Rasselas*, ed R. W. Chapman (Oxford, Clarendon Press, 1927).

Life—*Boswell's Life of Johnson*, ed. George Birkbeck Hill, revised by L. F. Powell, 6 vols. (Oxford, Clarendon Press, 1934—50).

INTRODUCTION

In 1878, in a short biography of Samuel Johnson, presumably devoted to re-establishing his reputation as an important man of letters after almost a century of neglect of Johnson's own writings by a public who preferred to be acquainted with Johnson through Boswell's *Life*, Sir Leslie Stephen directed his attention to Johnson's allegories in the *Rambler* long enough to remark,

Like Addison he indulges in allegory, which, in his hands, becomes unendurably frigid and clumsy.[1]

Some fifty years later, in a book presumably devoted to re-establishing Johnson's reputation as a major British essayist, O. F. Christie repeated Stephen's remark, added,

Tedious indeed are the personifications, and tedious their pedigrees, connections, and employments,[2]

and concluded,

in any volume of Johnson's selected essays I think it would be a mistake to insert specimens of the allegories.[3]

The various editors of the few collections of Johnson's selected works that have appeared in the last two decades seem, for the most part, to have quietly followed Christie's advice.

In Johnson's own time, the allegories were among the most popular and most frequently reprinted of his essays. The allegories in the *Rambler* seem to have caught the immediate attention of Johnson's public. An anonymous poem of praise "To the Author

[1] Leslie Stephen, *Samuel Johnson* (London, Macmillan & Co., 1878), p. 175.

[2] O. F. Christie, *Johnson The Essayist* (New York, George H. Doran Co., 1925), p. 123.

[3] Christie, p. 124.

of *The Rambler* On Reading his Allegories" was printed in the
Daily Advertiser of August 28, 1750, when only the first three of
Johnson's *Rambler* allegories (Nos. 3, 22, and 33) had appeared. In
1760, Bishop Percy, in a letter to Shenstone, singled out Johnson's
"Oriental Tales & Allegories" as "not the least striking productions
of his Pen'.[4] By the last decade of the century, a critic writing in
the *Looker-On* did not hesitate to list 'the author of the Rambler"
as one of the four English writers most renowned for composing
dream allegories, placing Johnson in the class of Spenser, Bunyan,
and Addison.[5]

One naturally is inclined to ask how Johnson's reputation as an
allegorist could have declined so greatly between the end of the
eighteenth century and the beginning of the twentieth. Much of
the answer must be that Johnson's general reputation as a writer
suffered in the nineteenth century. Boswell's *Life of Johnson* unfortunately had the effect, certainly never intended by its author,
of drawing attention away from Johnson's own works. As Professor James L. Clifford has pointed out, "Ironically, it was the
greatness of his disciple's art which for at least a century tended
to obscure Johnson's true stature . . . The Victorians were generally
content to take Johnson as a character out of a great book."[6]
It is not surprising, then, that Johnson's allegories were generally
overlooked in the nineteenth century. The question to be asked,
rather, is why, today, when Johnsonian scholars have for the past
several decades been taking a serious interest in Johnson's own
works, do they still pay so little critical attention to his allegories.[7]

The fact is that Johnson's allegories are often thought to be too
colorless, too transparent, for modern taste. One scholar who himself has the highest admiration for Johnson's allegorical "Vision of
Theodore", nevertheless finds it necessary to remark that "for

---

[4] Cited in note, *Life*, I, 537. It is in this letter that Percy reports that
Johnson considered "The Vision of Theodore" the best thing he ever wrote.

[5] *Looker-On* No. 22 (May 22, 1792), in *The British Essayists*, ed. A. Chal-
mers (London, 1817), XLI, 228—229.

[6] James L. Clifford, *Johnsonian Studies 1887—1950* (Minneapolis, University of Minnesota Press, 1951), p. 2.

[7] In 1965, there did appear a dissertation (University of Kansas) by
Harry Alan Ebeling entitled "The Allegorical Tales of Samuel Johnson".
The present study, the major portion of which was completed before that
time, is in no way indebted to Ebeling's work. See further note, p. 79.

modern readers the piece may be too sententious, too allegorical".[8] The implication may be that since Johnson's time allegorical and didactic writing in general has lost its appeal. But in recent decades, works of allegory have been receiving an increasing amount of attention from numerous 'modern readers'; yet Johnson's allegory remains neglected. It must be something in the nature of Johnsonian allegory in particular which causes its difficulty of reception.

The nature of Johnsonian allegory, of course, involves the nature of Johnsonian imagery, which has long been a subject of controversy among critics and scholars. Professor Donald Greene, with Bertrand Bronson's 'double tradition' of Johnson the man in mind,[9] recently has noted, "It is apparent that there has likewise existed a 'double tradition' of Johnson the writer — two quite contradictory ways of reading the words on a Johnsonian page. The one sees it as exuberant with concrete and vivid imagery; the other finds only a drear waste of 'abstraction' and inflated, pompous verbosity."[10] Professor Greene undoubtedly has observed a true phenomenon, and most literary critics can easily be placed in one tradition or the other. But he seems not to realize that just as both traditions of Johnson the man have their basis in something in the character of the man himself, so do both traditions of Johnson the writer stem from something which must be sought in the characteristics of Johnson's writing. The double tradition does not depend simply upon one's way of reading a Johnsonian page. If we read Johnson correctly we are somehow aware of, and should be responsive to, both the 'abstraction' and the 'concrete and vivid imagery' of his prose. And nowhere so much as in the allegories. For allegory by its nature employs the concrete to depict the abstract. Clearly neither of the 'two quite contradictory ways of reading the words on a Johnsonian page' which Greene recognizes

[8] James L. Clifford, *Young Sam Jonson* (New York, McGraw-Hill Book Company, Inc., 1955), p. 306.

[9] See Bertrand H. Bronson, "The Double Tradition of Dr. Johnson", in *Eighteenth-Century English Literature: Modern Essays in Criticism*, ed. James L. Clifford (New York, Oxford University Press, 1959) pp. 285—299. (Reprinted from *ELH*, June 1951.)

[10] Donald J. Greene, " 'Pictures To The Mind': Johnson And Imagery", in *Johnson, Boswell, and Their Circle: Essays Presented to L. F. Powell* (Oxford, Clarendon Press, 1965), p. 156.

will suffice for allegory. The primary aim of this study is to help
the reader to read properly the words on a page of Johnsonian
allegory.

  Each chapter of the following discussion, it is hoped, contributes
in some way to the attainment of this goal. My first chapter attempts
to show by an examination of Johnson's critical opinions that
Johnson found the form of allegory especially well suited to satisfying the aesthetic and moral demands he made of art. After a
brief second chapter designed to clarify the meaning of allegory
and certain related terms, my study turns in Chapter III to the
specific demands Johnson made of allegory, many of which help
to explain the peculiarities of Johnson's own allegorical technique.
The most striking characteristic of Johnson's allegorical technique,
his masterful use of the allegorical pun, is the subject of Chapter IV.
The subsequent chapters are devoted to critical analyses of each
of Johnson's allegorical works. Chapter V considers "The Vision
of Theodore", Johnson's earliest allegory and the one of which he
seems to have been most fond. Chapter VI is devoted to Johnson's
allegories in the *Rambler*, which also are used to provide the examples of allegorical puns in Chapter IV. Chapter VII considers several
'borderline cases', which, while not strictly allegorical, contain
definite elements of allegory, and in which can be found perhaps
some of the best examples of Johnson's allegorical technique. My
study concludes with a brief examination of *Rasselas* concerned specifically with the interpretation of the metaphor of the Happy
Valley.

I

JOHNSON AND POETIC FORM

1

Samuel Johnson possessed the powers of a poet. And he was aware
that those powers, "by which the understanding is enlightened,
or the imagination enchanted", with the single exception of the
art of versification, "may be exercised in prose".[1] The prose of
Samuel Johnson is a poet's prose: its art is that "of uniting pleasure
with truth, by calling imagination to the help of reason"; its end
"to instruct by pleasing".[2] But art and end to be realized must
find expression in form.

Form depends on – a better word than content – knowledge.
It is the word more appropriate to a discussion of Johnson's art
for his choice of form was determined, or if that is too strong
a word, influenced not by the stories he had to tell but by the
kind of knowledge he wished to convey.[3]

Almost all of Johnson's imaginative prose is in the form of allegory or contains elements of allegory. In one of the earliest critical
discussions of Johnson's prose, the Reverend Robert Burrowes
remarked,

His subjects . . . were such as scarcely could be treated of without figurative

---

[1] *Rambler* No. 86, *Works*, II, 404.

[2] "Life of Milton", *Lives*, I, 170; "Preface to Shakespeare", *Works*,
V, 111.

[3] I take the words 'knowledge' and 'form' in this context from Thomas
Mann, who wrote in an essay published near the end of his career, "The
principles which seem to me to delimit the existence of the poet and man
of letters are *knowledge* and *form*: these both at one and the same time".
The characteristic feature is, that for him these two, knowledge and form,
are an organic unit, in which each determines, requires, and produces the
other. ("The Artist and Society", in *The Study of Literature*, ed. Sylvan
Barnet *et al.*; Boston, Little, Brown & Co., 1960, pp. 253–254.)

diction: the powers of the understanding require the aid of illustration to become intelligible to common readers[4]

And a recent critical article has stated that "Johnson's temperament is one inherently conducive to an allegorical management of language".[5] But we need not rely on our knowledge of Johnson's subjects or temperament to explain why he found the form of allegory especially congenial. For an examination of Johnson's own critical remarks on the art and end of poetry makes it clear that Johnson looked upon allegory as a form particularly well suited to his aims.

Johnson is of all critics the most insistent that knowledge is necessary to the making of a poet. Johnson thought knowledge requisite to providing both pleasure and instruction, for he considered it as essential to the operation of the imagination as to the exercise of reason. "Imagination", he wrote, "is useless without knowledge: nature gives in vain the power of combination, unless study and observation supply materials to be combined".[6] In *Rasselas* Imlac enumerates the kinds of knowledge a poet must possess until the list becomes so long that Rasselas cries out, "Enough! Thou hast convinced me, that no human being can ever be a poet".[7] But if Johnson shared Imlac's belief that ideally a poet must know everything, he did not feel a poet must tell everything he knows. "To a poet nothing can be useless";[8] in a poem much may be, and a good deal of it pernicious besides. "The poet's art is selection."[9] If his aim is moral instruction, it is his responsibility to select from his store of knowledge that which will make men better.

Not every kind of knowledge is certain to result in the furtherance of morality. "That observation which is called knowledge of the world", for example, "will be found much more frequently to make men cunning than good".[10] Johnson acknowledges that it is the

[4] Robert Burrowes, "Essay on the Stile of Doctor Samuel Johnson", No. II (November 13, 1786), *The Transactions of the Royal Irish Academy* (Dublin, 1787), p. 49.

[5] E. San Juan, Jr., "The Actual and the Ideal in Johnson's *Dictionary*", *University of Toronto Quarterly*, XXXIV (January, 1965), 155.

[6] "Life of Butler", *Lives*, I, 212.

[7] *Rasselas*, p. 52.

[8] *Rasselas*, p. 50.

[9] "Life of Shenstone", *Lives*, III, 356.

[10] *Rambler* No. 4, *Works*, II, 18.

excellence of art to imitate nature, but not without warning "it is necessary to distinguish those parts of nature which are most proper for imitation".[11] The poet has the right, and also the duty, to take advantage of the fact that art is NOT nature. Johnson expresses his view early in the *Rambler:*

> If the world be promiscuously described, I cannot see of what use it can be to read the account; or why it may not be as safe to turn the eye immediately upon mankind as upon a mirror which shows all that presents itself without discrimination.
>
> It is, therefore, not a sufficient vindication of a character, that it is drawn as it appears; for many characters ought never to be drawn . . .[12]

For such offenses, Johnson repeatedly blamed Shakespeare. Of the faults Johnson finds with Shakespeare – 'faults sufficient to obscure and overwhelm any other merit' – the major one is, after all, that he imitates nature too well:

> . . . he makes no just distribution of good or evil, nor is always careful to show in the virtuous a disapprobation of the wicked; he carries his persons indifferently through right and wrong, and, at the close, dismisses them without further care, and leaves their examples to operate by chance.[13]

For Johnson, Shakespeare's faithfulness to nature is a neglect of the responsibility of art, "for it is always a writer's duty to make the world better". Shakespeare's is a common sin of omission:

> His first defect is that to which may be imputed most of the evil in books or in men. He sacrifices virtue to convenience, and is so much more careful to please than to instruct, that he seems to write without any moral purpose.[14]

Johnson is not simply blaming Shakespeare for failing to observe the principle of 'poetical justice'. For Johnson readily granted that "since wickedness often prospers in real life, the poet is certainly at liberty to give it prosperity on the stage".[15] What Johnson objects to in Shakespeare's plays is not that virtue and vice do not receive their proper rewards but that they are frequently so intricately combined that neither can be clearly seen.

[11] *Works*, II, 18.
[12] *Works*, II, 18.
[13] "Preface to Shakespeare", *Works*, V, 115.
[14] *Works*, V, 115.
[15] "Life of Addison", *Lives*, II, 135.

To write with a moral purpose does not mean for Johnson that an author must tell only of virtue rewarded. Vice must be shown, and may even be shown to prosper. But it must be shown in such a way that it does not receive approbation. Johnson explains in *Rambler* No. 4,

Vice, for vice is necessary to be shown, should always disgust; nor should the graces of gaiety, or the dignity of courage, be so united with it, as to reconcile it to the mind. Wherever it appears, it should raise hatred by the malignity of its practices, and contempt by the meanness of its stratagems: for while it is supported by either parts or spirit, it will be seldom heartily abhorred.[16]

The writer, then, must exhibit vice only in its 'purity'. "He that instructs must offer to the mind something to be imitated or something to be avoided", not something in between.[17] When virtue is to be shown,[18] Johnson's attitude is similar:

In narratives, where historical veracity has no place, I cannot discover why there should not be exhibited the most perfect idea of virtue; of virtue not angelical, nor above probability, ... but the highest and purest that humanity can reach ...[19]

The opening qualification must of course be taken into consideration in order to understand properly Johnson's position. Johnson's remarks in *Rambler* No. 4 are concerned specifically with works of romantic fiction, "written chiefly to the young, the ignorant, and the idle, to whom they serve as lectures of conduct, and introductions into life".[20] But we must remember too that Johnson's own periodical essays, if not directed chiefly to such readers, were designed to serve a similar purpose.

Nevertheless, it should be understood that where 'historical veracity' has a place, Johnson has the highest regard for it. He especially esteems the art of biography and often recommends it for its moral applicability. "Biography", he says in *Idler* No. 84, "is, of

[16] *Rambler* No. 4, *Works*, II, 20.
[17] *Idler* No. 97, *Idler and Adventurer*, p. 298.
[18] And it is to be shown: Johnson writes in *Rambler* No. 50, "I have always thought it the business of those who turn their speculations upon the living world, to commend the virtues, as well as to expose the faults of their contemporaries". (*Works*, II, 240.)
[19] *Rambler* No. 4, *Works*, II, 19—20.
[20] *Works*, II, 16.

the various kinds of narrative writing, that which is most eagerly read, and most easily applied to the purposes of life".[21] But the problems of a biographer are of a kind different from those of the poet. The biographer or historian is obligated to facts: "the manners and actions of his personages are already fixed".[22] "The difficulty of making variety consistent . . . needs not to disturb him"[23] for he has the advantage of being enabled to express directly to the reader his disapprobation of wickedness in whatever combination it occurs. If ever there was an account of a man in whom vices are united with 'parts' and 'spirit', it is Johnson's own *Life of Savage*. But in it Johnson continually tells his reader in what Savage is to be emulated and where his example is to be avoided, for such is the biographer's privilege.

The poet's art must speak for itself. His obligation is to extract a vice or a virtue from its mixed surroundings so that its true nature may be seen, and seen at once. The metaphor of extraction is Johnson's own:

gold may be so concealed in baser matter that only a chymist can recover it; sense may be so hidden in unrefined and plebeian words that none but philosophers can distinguish it; and both may be so buried in impurities as not to pay the cost of their extraction.[24]

But to extract a human quality is to abstract it: to present the general rather than the particular. As Imlac states in his dissertation upon poetry, part of the task of a poet is to "consider right and wrong in their abstracted and invariable state".[25] The poet must, in short, possess the quality of 'Judgement', which "by separating the essence of things from its concomitants", Johnson tells us in the *Life of Pope*, "often makes the representation more powerful than the reality".[26]

This is not to say that the realistic forms of fictional representation are necessarily closed to the moral writer. Johnson has no fault to find, to take but one example, with Shakespeare's dramatic

---

[21] *Idler and Adventurer*, p. 261.

[22] *Rambler* No. 122, *Works*, III. 82.

[23] *Works*, III, 82.

[24] "Life of Cowley", *Lives*, I, 59.

[25] *Rasselas*, p. 50.

[26] *Lives*, III, 247.

presentation of the character of Iago. Here, for once, Shakespeare
has not failed to meet his moral responsibility:

> There is always danger, lest wickedness, conjoined with abilities, should
> steal upon esteem, though it misses of approbation; but the character of
> Iago is so conducted, that he is from the first scene to the last hated and
> despised.[27]

But it must be added that Shakespeare's Iago is not an ordinary
realistic character. A recent study has brilliantly shown the evolu-
tionary kinship between Iago and the figure of Vice in the traditional morality play.[28] It is no coincidence that Johnson found one
of Shakespeare's most allegorical characters the least morally equi-
vocal. Nevertheless Johnson attributed Shakespeare's apparent
moral lapses to negligence rather than to the demands of dramatic
realism. He was convinced that most forms of literature, whatever
their particular requirements, could satisfactorily serve the end of
moral instruction. But a poet-and-critic, let us hope, will tolerate
more forms than he uses. For his own writings, Johnson sought
the forms which would enable him to convey moral knowledge in
the surest and most economical way.

Johnson found allegory suited to his purpose because it enables
the writer to show vice and virtue unalloyed. By presenting human
qualities abstracted from particular instances, it frees him from the
obligation that more realistic forms might impose of depicting the
'unessential and casual varieties' by which "the interests and passions, the virtues and vices of mankind, have been diversified in
different times".[29] Johnson wished to insure that no such 'varieties'
would obscure the essential nature of the human qualities he described. As Professor Bronson explains, "an artist sure of what he
wishes to say about the nature of the ordered, ideal world will
not wait for chance and our random inclinations to lead us to his
meaning".[30]

[27] Johnson, *Notes to Shakespeare*, ed. Arthur Sherbo, Augustan Reprint
Society Publication No. 73 (Los Angeles, University of California, 1958),
p. 201.

[28] Bernard Spivack, *Shakespeare and the Allegory of Evil* (New York,
Columbia University Press, 1958).

[29] *Adventurer* No. 95, *Idler and Adventurer*, p. 425.

[30] Bertrand H. Bronson, "Personification Reconsidered", in *New Light
On Dr. Johnson*, ed. Frederick W. Hilles (New Haven, Yale University Press,
1959), p. 213.

2

But a poet must instruct BY PLEASING. He has aesthetic as well as moral obligations. Johnson found allegory a form of expression well suited to the purpose of moral instruction. It remains to be shown that he found it also suited to the purpose of pleasing. But if the moral advantage of the form is its capability of depicting the pure and the general, might that not also be its aesthetic advantage? It would seem almost too easy a task to show that Johnson found the general more aesthetically pleasing than the particular. It is common enough to say that such a preference is a defining characteristic of eighteenth-century sensibility. A critic would have only to bring together Johnson's several assertions of 'the grandeur of generality' and declare how well he reflected his age. And many critics have done so. The trouble is that those statements which have so often been quoted indicate neither the invariable opinion of his age nor of Johnson. His opinion was not that of his age, unless by the opinion of his age we mean whatever Johnson thought. And what he thought is not revealed by a few scattered remarks in praise of generality. The truth is that Johnson, more often than not, found generality displeasing. Like another periodical-writer of the eighteenth century, he was inclined to feel, "there is nothing in nature so irksome as general discourses".[31]

Recent critics of course are aware that Johnson's aesthetic position has been misunderstood. Walter Jackson Bate admits that it was misunderstood by him as late as 1946.[32] The view that Johnson was the champion of generality in art was by no means a prejudice that died with the nineteenth century. Only in recent years has Johnson's criticism been looked at freshly. The later studies of Professor Bate, and those of Professors Hagstrum and Keast, have tried to show that Johnson's critical theory is more complex than had been thought. It is, but not so complex as they have made it. Professor Bate claims that Johnson's position "avoids the usual

---

[31] Joseph Addison, The Spectator (No. 267), ed. George A. Aitken (London, George Routledge & Sons, Ltd.), III, 249.

[32] W. J. Bate, The Achievement of Samuel Johnson (New York, Oxford University Press, 1955), p. 199 and p. 240, n. 30. Bate declares himself guilty of having used Imlac's statement that a poet must 'rise to general and transcendental truths' as a key to Johnson's critical (i.e. aesthetic) thought in his From Classic to Romantic (1946).

monotonous quarrel over the issue of generality versus particularity in art . . . by subsuming it within a larger framework". He suggests that the generality Johnson desires is "a species of symbolic value; it proceeds through the concrete detail, but the test is still how applicable it is beyond".[33] Professor Hagstrum has it just the other way around: "Johnson wanted the general to recall the particular."[34] Professor Keast, as if by way of compromise, asserts that Johnson derived pleasure "neither from the merely particular nor the merely general".[35] Each of the three statements is somehow true, but that is no comfort to the student who would like to know why Johnson spoke sometimes as if he found generality pleasing and sometimes as if he did not.

Part of the answer, to be sure, is that Johnson's responses to literature were fresh, immediate, and honest and that he refused to let himself be trapped by a system. Johnson objected to "the cant of those who judge by principles rather than perception".[36] But he directed such objections primarily against "such readers as draw their principles of judgement rather from books than from reason",[37] not against principles themselves. It is by no means a fruitless task to seek the reasonable principles which underlie and guide Johnson's critical perceptions. It is unfortunate that the combined effect of the efforts of Bate, Hagstrum, and Keast has been further to obscure Johnson's position. Their three studies, oddly enough, share to varying extents the same defect: they lose sight of the fact that Johnson's aesthetic and moral criteria for judging a work of art are not the same. It does not follow that by meeting one set of requirements the artist will automatically meet the other. Both must be satisfied in the same work at the same time, but not in the same way.

When Johnson has Imlac say, "The business of a poet . . . is to examine, not the individual, but the species; to remark general

[33] Bate, p. 199.

[34] Jean H. Hagstrum, *Samuel Johnson's Literary Criticism* (Minneapolis, University of Minnesota Press, 1952), p. 88.

[35] William R. Keast, "Johnson's Criticism of the Metaphysical Poets", in *Eighteenth-Century English Literature: Modern Essays in Criticism*, ed. James L. Clifford (New York, Oxford University Press, 1959), p. 307. (Reprinted from *ELH*, March 1950.)

[36] "Life of Pope", *Lives*, III, 248.

[37] "Life of Milton", *Lives*, I, 176.

properties and large appearances", he means to define the MORAL business of a poet.[38] It is not a rewarding business. Imlac makes it clear that he who wishes to "rise to general and transcendental truths" must "contemn the applause of his own time".[39] Generality is not of itself pleasing, and, what is more, neither is truth. Johnson says as much in *Rambler* No. 96:

> Truth is, indeed, not often welcome for its own sake; it is generally unpleasing . . .[40]

The poet's art is to UNITE pleasure with truth because they so often occur apart:

> For this reason many arts of instruction have been invented, by which the reluctance against truth may be overcome; and as physick is given to children in confections, precepts have been hidden under a thousand appearances, that mankind may be bribed by pleasure to escape destruction.[41]

'The insipidity of truth' and 'the stability of truth' are, alike, phrases from Johnson's "Preface to Shakespeare".[42] It was not Johnson who said truth is beauty. He surely obtained no aesthetic pleasure from his religion, which he accepted as the highest truth. Indeed he argued that Christian poetry could hardly exist:

> Contemplative piety, or the intercourse between God and the human soul, cannot be poetical.[43]

Nothing provides better evidence of the division in Johnson's mind between the moral and aesthetic realms.

When Johnson calls for generality in art it is usually for reasons other than aesthetic. Only in the "Preface to Shakespeare", where he attempts to discover the reasons for Shakespeare's continued appeal, does he seem clearly to indicate that generality is itself a source of pleasure. Here Johnson confidently states, "Nothing can please many and please long, but just representations of general nature".[44] It would be merely quibbling to argue that Johnson said 'just', not 'general' representations, or to plead, with Hagstrum,

---

[38] *Rasselas*, p. 50.
[39] *Rasselas*, p. 51.
[40] *Works*, II, 454.
[41] *Rambler* No. 96, *Works*, II, 454—455.
[42] *Works*, V, 125, 105.
[43] "Life of Waller", *Lives*, I, 291.
[44] *Works*, V, 105.

that a just representation of the general recalls the particular, or, with Bate, that a particular representation, if just, suggests the general. Johnson did not mean that the general pleases by virtue of the particular. A better way must be found of reconciling his statement with the many in his criticism that appear to contradict it. In the Preface itself it is precisely when Shakespeare departs from generality that Johnson declares him "more careful to please than to instruct". How then may generality be called pleasing?

Johnson far more often finds the general unaffecting and therefore unpleasing. He typically complains (of the plays of Nicholas Rowe), "all is general and undefined. Nor does he much interest or affect the auditor",[45] or (of epitaphs), "The praise ought not to be general, because the mind is lost in the extent of any indefinite idea, and cannot be affected with what it cannot comprehend."[46] Is it possible that what pleases many does not please much? (We may recall Johnson's remark, "what is fit for every thing can fit nothing well".)[47] A perfectly clear answer is given by Johnson in *Idler* No. 59:

> He that writes upon general principles, or delivers universal truths, may hope to be often read, because his work will be equally useful at all times and in every country, but he cannot expect it to be received with eagerness, or to spread with rapidity, because desire can have no particular stimulation; that which is to be loved long must be loved with reason rather than with passion.[48]

If we re-examine Johnson's statement that "nothing can please many and please long, but just representations of general nature", we will find that the key words are 'many' and 'long'. Shakespeare has pleased succeeding generations of men by concentrating on the general nature common to them all. The particular and the timely may certainly be more pleasing to a selected audience, for they have the greater power of affecting. But the timely, by nature, cannot be timely long.

---

[45] *Lives*, II, 76.

[46] "Essay on Epitaphs", *Works*, V, 264. That Johnson's censure pertains not only to the writing of epitaphs is made clear by the preceding sentence: "In drawing the character of the deceased, there are no rules to be observed which do not equally relate to other compositions."

[47] "Life of Cowley", *Lives*, I, 47.

[48] *Idler and Adventurer*, pp. 183—184.

That is not to say that art has no place for it. Johnson considered it a legitimate aim of the writer to depict the manners of his age. In *Adventurer* No. 95, he inquires "by what arts are the writers of the present and future ages to attract the notice and favour of mankind", and determines, "they are to observe the alterations which time is always making in the modes of life, that they may gratify every generation with a picture of themselves".[49] But what he suggests to 'the writers of the present and future ages' is not what Johnson wants from the writers of the past. A writer may gratify his contemporaries with pictures of themselves; he will please posterity only with representations of general nature. Johnson does not have a different standard for judging the writers of the present and the writers of the past. He makes the same demand of both: that their representations have relevance FOR HIM. That is what any reader asks, and that is why "it often happens, that an author's reputation is endangered in succeeding times, by that which raised the loudest applause among his contemporaries".[50] Such was the case, Johnson felt, with Abraham Cowley:

He saw a certain way to present praise; and not sufficiently enquiring by what means the ancients have continued to delight through all the changes of human manners he contented himself with a deciduous laurel, of which the verdure in its spring was bright and gay, but which time has been continually stealing from his brows.[51]

The same work may be pertinent to its age and to the future, but, again, not in the same way. In Shakespeare much is topical; it pleased the Elizabethans, was missed by Johnson, and is obscure to us. What is general, to be sure, was as available to the Elizabethans as to ourselves, but their attention must often have been elsewhere. In the Preface to Shakespeare, Johnson fixes his attention upon the general because he is concerned only with explaining how Shakespeare's popularity has outlasted his age. Johnson attributed Shakespeare's permanence to his generality; modern critics prefer to call it universality. It is still Johnson's explanation. But, for Johnson, he who pleases by virtue of generality "must be loved with reason rather than with passion". In such a way must Shakespeare be loved by us however passionately he may have pleased the Elizabethans.

[49] *Idler and Adventurer*, p. 427.
[50] *Idler* No. 70, *Idler and Adventurer*, p. 217.
[51] "Life of Cowley", *Lives*, I, 56.

Not many a writer will have the ability to please, even in different ways, both his own age and ages to come. Most writers court the favor either of their contemporaries or of posterity. But their choice is not an undetermined one. For a writer directs himself to a selected audience by his subject. And subject, like form, is determined by knowledge. The Rambler answers readers who would have him treat their favorite subject by informing them that "an author has a rule of choice peculiar to himself; and selects those subjects which he is best qualified to treat, by the course of his studies, or the accidents of his life".[52] Of all writers, the periodical-essayist might with greatest justice try to gain the favor of his audience with timely subjects. Yet Johnson never did. He could report in the last of his Ramblers, "I have never complied with temporary curiosity, nor enabled my readers to discuss the topick of the day".[53] Johnson's subject was morality, for that was what he knew, not what he thought would please. The Rambler presumed he had "never been much a favourite of the publick".[54] Johnson's essays were directed to those "whose passions left them leisure for abstracted truth, and whom virtue could please by its naked dignity".[55] Johnson was willing to be loved with reason rather than with passion.

But to be loved at all, a writer, whether he discusses universal morality or the topic of the day, must give to his compositions one excellence "without which all others are of small avail, the power of engaging attention and alluring curiosity".[56] The curiosity Johnson has in mind is that 'restless and unquenchable curiosity' which a writer must excite if he would compel "him that reads his work to read it through".[57] The few aesthetic demands which Johnson felt literature must satisfy are perhaps best summarized in the following passage from the *Life of Dryden*:

Works of the imagination excel by their allurement and delight; by their power of attracting and detaining the attention. That book is good in vain which the reader throws away. He only is the master who keeps the mind

---

[52] *Rambler* No. 23, *Works*, II, 117.
[53] *Rambler* No. 208, *Works*, III, 462.
[54] *Works*, III, 461.
[55] *Rambler* No. 208, *Works*, III, 462.
[56] "Life of Prior", *Lives*, II, 206.
[57] "Preface to Shakespeare", *Works*, V, 126.

in pleasing captivity; whose pages are perused with eagerness, and in hope of new pleasure are perused again; and whose conclusion is perceived with an eye of sorrow, such as the traveller casts upon departing day.[58]

The subject of a work may stimulate the desire of a reader enough for him to pick it up, but he can as easily throw it down once it fails to delight. "Tediousness is the most fatal of all faults . . ."[59] And one of the most common. The general and the particular alike can become tedious in the hands of a dull writer.

Only those qualities by which tediousness is counteracted are of themselves pleasing. Novelty and variety are for Johnson the prime sources of pleasure. He says so everywhere in his criticism, but always in passing, as if he considers it self-evident. It may be for that reason that Johnson's extended discussions of generality have more often detained the attention of his critics. But the generality or particularity of a work is more likely to determine who is pleased by it than how it pleases. The immediate concern of Johnson's practical criticism is with the means by which a writer may enliven his compositions. Such assertions as the following can hardly be missed, but their very prevalence has made them unobtrusive:

The great source of pleasure is variety.
. . . novelty is the great source of pleasure.
. . . upon the whole, all pleasure consists in variety.
The pleasures of the mind imply something sudden and unexpected; that which elevates must always surprise.
. . . he that pleases must offer new images to his reader . . .[60]

The first two statements are not contradictory. Johnson can refer to both variety and novelty as THE great source of pleasure because he looks upon each as a source of the other. For Johnson, who shared with his age the view that there was under the sun very little that was new, novelty is produced by varying the old. New images are only new associations, for imagination is "the power of combination".[61] That new images, in turn, ADD variety to a piece is, of course, obvious.

[58] *Lives*, I, 454.
[59] "Life of Prior", *Lives*, II, 206.
[60] "Life of Butler", *Lives*, I, 212; "Life of Prior", *Lives*, II, 206; "Preface to Shakespeare", *Works*, V, 111; "Life of Cowley", *Lives*, I, 59; *Idler* No. 97, *Idler and Adventurer*, p. 298.
[61] "Life of Butler", *Lives*, I, 212.

Johnson, then, if his own works were to please, had to fill them with novelty and variety. But he had to find a means of doing so that would not detract from his primary purpose of moral instruction. It is not surprising that Johnson often turned to allegory, which he remarks in *Rambler* No. 121 "is perhaps one of the most pleasing vehicles of instruction".[62] Allegory conveys abstract truth, but conveys it through the concreteness of fiction. By such a union of the concrete and the abstract Johnson sought to enable the mind, at once, to feast upon "the luxurious wonders of fiction" and "repose on the stability of truth".[63]

[62] *Works*, III, 79.
[63] "Preface to Shakespeare", *Works*, V, 125, 105.

II

ALLEGORY AND ALLEGORICAL METAPHOR

The difficulty of defining literary forms is acknowledged by Johnson in *Rambler* No. 125, where he declares,

> There is ... scarcely any species of writing, of which we can tell what is its essence, and what are its constituents; every new genius produces some innovation, which, when invented and approved, subverts the rules which the practice of foregoing authors had established.[1]

Furthermore, in his "Preface to the English Dictionary", Johnson remarks,

> When the nature of things is unknown, or the notion unsettled and indefinite, and various in various minds, the words by which such notions are conveyed, or such things denoted, will be ambiguous and perplexed.[2]

The notion of allegory is indeed "various in various minds". Those critics who are most concerned with the subject have reached little agreement on the meaning of the term. There is no accepted definition of allegory, and it is not within the scope of this study to attempt to supply one.[3] But before proceeding to discuss Samuel Johnson's allegories, a critic is obliged at least to state what he means by allegory. What follows is not a definition of allegory designed to suit all needs, but rather an explanation of what I understand by the term.

---

[1] *Works*, III, 93.

[2] *Works*, V, 34.

[3] The most comprehensive discussion of the nature of allegory may be found in Professor Angus Fletcher's *Allegory: The Theory of a Symbolic Mode* (Ithaca, Cornell University Press, 1964). But the very breadth of Fletcher's study makes it not especially helpful in determining what is an allegory and what is not. According to Fletcher, "we must be ready to discern in almost any work at least a small degree of allegory". (p. 8.)

It is clear that allegory is not a genre. Allegory may occur in verse or prose, epic or essay. Yet allegory is properly called a form, for it is clearly a way of ordering the matter of literature. It may be best to avoid any possible confusion of form and genre by speaking of allegory for the time being as a mode of expression. Clearly, it is a metaphorical mode of expression. The traditional rhetoric-book definition of allegory as an extended metaphor is still not a bad one. The only difficulty is that modern criticism is no longer so sure of the meaning of metaphor. C. S. Lewis, revealingly, has reversed the classical formula to "every metaphor is an allegory in little".[4] Allegory is now often looked upon as the more fixed, at least the more confined, of the two terms. For many critics have come to view metaphor as the basic element of all poetic language. The word, replacing 'symbol' and 'myth' as the critical catchword of the day, has become 'ambiguous and perplexed'.

Before we ceased to know what metaphor means, Aristotle's definition usually sufficed. According to his *Poetics*, "Metaphor consits in giving the thing a name that belongs to something else; the transference being either from genus to species, or from species to genus, or from species to species, or on grounds of analogy."[5] The trouble with Aristotle's definition is only that it fails to account for implicit metaphor. Instead of 'giving the thing a name' a writer may merely use a verb that personifies. One could defend Aristotle's definition by arguing that in such a case it is the act the verb signifies which is given a name that belongs to something else. But more usually, at least in literary criticism, we mean by metaphor the analogy established rather than the word used to establish it. Professor William York Tindall refers to metaphor as "an analogy" which "may take the form of an equation of stated elements or an image by which one term is presented while the other remains implicit".[6] Johnson, recognizing metaphor as an analogy, calls it in his *Dictionary*, "a simile comprized in a word", although his

[4] C. S. Lewis, *The Allegory of Love* (London, Oxford University Press, 1936), p, 60.

[5] Aristotle, *Basic Works*, ed. Richard McKeon (New York, Random House, 1941), p. 1476. Aristotle's definition is broad enough to include the trope that later rhetoricians distinguished from metaphor and called synecdoche. Aristotle was probably more right in viewing it as a category of metaphor.

[6] William York Tindall, *The Literary Symbol* (New York, Columbia University Press, 1955), p. 35.

primary definition is not far removed from Aristotle's: Johnson first records that metaphor is "the application of a word to an use to which, in its original import, it cannot be put". But even Aristotle comes close to our conception of metaphor as an analogy between basically dissimilar elements when he prescribes that "metaphor must be by transference from things that are related, but not obviously so, as it is a sign of sound intuition in a philosopher to see similarities between things that are far apart".[7]

Today "metaphor is everywhere acknowledged as the core of poetic statement".[8] Statements which once would have sounded like definitions of allegory are now made about poetry in general: "Poetry provides the one permissible way of saying one thing and meaning another" (Robert Frost). "A poem should be equal to: Not true" (Archibald Mac Leish). As a result, Johnson's definition of allegory as "a figurative discourse, in which something other is intended, than is contained in the words literally taken"[9] no longer seems to tell us how allegory differs from the rest of literature. Even so, it has fared better than that of Coleridge, for whom "an allegory is but a translation of abstract notions into a picture-language . . .".[10] It is now difficult to see how Coleridge has distinguished allegory from much of language itself. C. S. Lewis says, "It is of the very nature of thought and language to represent what is immaterial in picturable terms."[11]

If metaphor is the 'core' of literature, all literature must be conceived of as something close to extended metaphor. But not all metaphors are alike. If we can still speak of allegory as a form of literature different from any other, we are able to do so because allegory employs a particular kind of metaphor. Allegory can be exactly defined only as a system or pattern of 'allegorical' metaphors.[12] The typical example of the allegorical metaphor is the per-

[7] *Rhetoric*, III, ii, Aristotle, *On Poetry and Style*, trans G. M. A. Grube (New York, Liberal Arts Press, 1958), p. 93.

[8] Bertrand H. Bronson, "Personification Reconsidered", in *New Light On Dr. Johnson*, ed. Frederick W. Hilles (New Haven, Yale University Press, 1959), p. 194.

[9] *Dictionary*.

[10] Samuel Taylor Coleridge, *The Statesman's Manual* (1816), *Complete Works*, ed. W. G. T. Shedd (New York, Harper & Brothers, 1884), I, 437.

[11] *The Allegory of Love*, p. 44.

[12] I do not mean to be circular. By 'allegorical metaphor' I mean no more than 'the kind of metaphor that occurs in allegory'. At this stage of my

sonification, or personified abstraction. The latter is the more fully
accurate term. For not all personifications are of abstractions and
only those that are are examples of allegorical metaphor. Professor
Bertrand Bronson uses the categories 'abstract-personification' and
'object-personification' to distinguish the two kinds.[13] He would
do better, though, to label the second category simply 'non-
abstract personification', for a figure – Mother Earth, for example –
is sometimes both an abstraction and an object. The thing personified does not have to be intangible in order to be abstract. 'Personified abstraction' would almost define allegorical metaphor
except that the word 'personified' is unnecessarily restrictive. It
makes no essential difference in a metaphor whether an abstract
concept is embodied in a person or in a mountain, river, castle, lion,
or rose. A valley named Despair is a figure of the same kind as
a giant named Despair.

My example points to the first of the characteristics by which
allegorical metaphor may be differentiated from symbol, or – if
symbol is a species of metaphor – symbolic metaphor: in an allegorical metaphor the 'vehicle' is arbitrary.[14] Despair may be pictured as a giant or a valley according to the allegorist's whim; the
particular embodiment he decides upon is only one of several possibilities. The symbol is usually thought to be less separable from
what it suggests. William York Tindall goes so far as to say, "The
symbol is the only possible embodiment of what it presents."[15]
If for Professor Tindall's 'what it presents', could be substituted
'ALL THE THINGS it presents', no one would quarrel with the statement. For the second important way in which symbol and allegorical metaphor are different is that a symbol has multiple and
indefinite meanings, whereas the 'tenor' of an allegorical metaphor
is fixed. It is not necessary to insist upon a one-to-one correspon-
dence between image and idea as a defining characteristic of allegory. An allegorical figure can easily be subject to two interpreta-

---

argument, the word 'allegorical' has no content; I use it only to avoid a
clumsy phrase.

[13] Bronson, in *New Light*, p. 199.

[14] I follow a number of modern critics in referring to the two parts of a
metaphor as 'tenor' and 'vehicle'. I believe the terms were used first by
I. A. Richards.

[15] *The Literary Symbol*, p. 31.

tions – usually one religious and one political – and still have definite reference. But an allegorist will rarely manage more meanings than two or three and remain an allegorist. The third difference between allegorical metaphor and symbol is generally the cause of the second; in a symbolic metaphor the tenor is always left unstated. With allegorical metaphors, that may be the case, but most often the figures are given names which immediately identify the concepts they stand for. (A Tale of a Tub is an example of an allegory in which the tenor of the metaphors is unstated, although the significance of the names Peter, Martin, and Jack is obvious to most readers.)

Two other distinctions between allegory and symbol which are often put forth, I find unconvincing. The first is that the allegorist more than the symbolist views his fiction 'merely' as a vehicle that exists for the meaning beyond it. The view has been expressed by Allen Tate, for one. He writes of allegorical images, "they stand, not in themselves, but merely for something else".[16] I do not know that this is less true of symbols. Why else have symbols if not for what they symbolize? Or to put it the other way around, why should an allegorist create an image if it merely stands for an idea that can be expressed as well without it? A second widely accepted distinction between allegorist and symbolist has been given expression by C. S. Lewis. He argues, "The difference between the two can hardly be exaggerated. The allegorist leaves the given – his own passions – to talk of that which is confessedly less real, which is fiction. The symbolist leaves the given to find that which is more real."[17] In other words, the allegorist, starting with the immaterial, produces a concrete fiction, while the symbolist proceeds from the concrete to spiritual reality. Who knows? It is not something that can be discovered by reading a work. Lewis's position involves an 'intentional fallacy', or something very much like one. Furthermore Lewis promotes the feeling that allegory and symbolism are opposites. Bronson rightly answers, "The true opposite of allegory is naturalism" (i.e. not to use metaphors at all).[18] Allegorical and symbolic metaphor may often occur in the same work. Lewis's

---

[16] Allen Tate, *Collected Essays* (Denver, Alan Swallow, 1959), p. 97.
[17] *The Allegory of Love*, p. 45.
[18] Bronson, in *New Light*, p. 209.

point of view prevents him from seeing that Dante was both symbolist and allegorist.

An allegorical metaphor can now be defined as a metaphor by which one (or rarely more than one) specific abstract concept is explicitly or implicitly embodied in a figure (person or thing) with which it has no necessary connection.[19] It needs only to be added that a figure may exist within a figure. A castle may represent Wealth and its door Temptation. In such a case, castle and castle door would each be a separate allegorical metaphor. If, on the other hand, a castle represents Knowledge and its doorway Education, we begin to have a system of allegorical metaphors. Two abstractions are not only pictured, but their relationship is indicated: Education is the doorway to Knowledge. For such a system, by which a number of allegorical metaphors are related to each other, I would reserve the name allegory.[20]

Neither the presence of narrative nor extensive length is a defining characteristic of allegory.[21] Johnson, in his *Dictionary*, illustrates the word by an allegory one sentence long: "Wealth is the daughter of diligence, and the parent of authority." The allegory is not especially picturesque, but by the use of metaphor, three abstract

---

[19] The type of metaphor found in Dryden's *Absalom and Achitophel*, whereby instead of an abstract concept a specific person or event is represented by another, must be separately accounted for. The use of such metaphor is properly called parody. Parody does not have to be humorous. It should be recognized as a special case of allegory.

[20] Mr. Paul Pickrel, in defining allegory, states, "It presents a group of vehicles (things expressed) corresponding to a group of tenors (things behind the things expressed), and the vehicles stand for a pattern of relationship and (usually) engage in a pattern of activity corresponding to a like pattern of activity among the tenors." (Cited by Ellen Douglass Leyburn, *Satiric Allegory*, p. 5, n. 6.) I find no fault with Mr. Pickrel's definition except that it does not distinguish the specific character of allegorical vehicles and tenors.

[21] The point is made by Ellen Douglass Leyburn. She writes, "There can, I think, be no justification for making narrative a criterion of allegory, though certainly many allegories have depended on the representing of one series of actions in terms of another. Nor can length be considered essential, though many allegories are long." Professor Leyburn defines allegory as "the particular method of saying one thing in terms of another in which two levels of meaning are sustained and in which the two levels correspond in pattern of relationship among details." (*Satiric Allegory*, pp. 5—6.)

concepts are embodied in persons and their relationship is shown.[22] Johnson is justified in recognizing the sentence as an allegory. An allegory may be coextensive with a work of literature or only a part of one. We refer to a work as AN allegory when allegory comprises either the major portion of it or the whole.

[22] In this instance, three allegorical figures are created by the metaphorical use of only two words, but that is due to the nature of the words 'daughter' and 'parent'.

III

JOHNSON ON ALLEGORY

In Mark Twain's *Tom Sawyer Abroad,* Huck Finn recounts the following dialogue between Tom Sawyer and Jim. Jim speaks first:

"Mars Tom, what is a metaphor?"

"A metaphor's a – well, it's a – a – a metaphor's an illustration." He see *that* didn't git home, so he tried again. "When I say birds of a feather flocks together, it's a metaphorical way of saying –"

"But dey *don't,* Mars Tom. No, sir, 'deed dey don't. Dey ain't no feathers dat's more alike den a bluebird en a jaybird, but ef you waits till you catches *dem* birds together, you'll –"[1]

Samuel Johnson did not have to ask what a metaphor is. But to the readers of his criticism he has often sounded as thick-headed as Jim for he had no patience with metaphors that are in any way foolish or inexact. Most metaphors do not stand up very well under close examination, and Johnson always examined metaphors closely.

In his notes to Shakespeare, Johnson finds two things wrong with the lines from *A Midsummer-Night's Dream,*

> – With doubler tongue
> Than thine, O serpent, never adder stung:
> (III, ii, 72 – 73.)

(1) adders do not sting with their tongues; (2) their tongues are not forked.[2] Johnson knew what a metaphor is. He understood

---

[1] Mark Twain, *Tom Sawyer Abroad* (New York, Collier Books, 1962), p. 48.

[2] Johnson, *Notes to Shakespeare,* ed. Arthur Sherbo, Augustan Reprint Society Publication No. 59 (Los Angeles, University of California, 1956), p. 34 (note to *Measure For Measure,* III, i, 16). Snakes, as far as I know, do have forked tongues, but Johnson considered the belief a 'vulgar notion'.

that in the play Hermia is addressing Demetrius as a serpent metaphorically and means that Demetrius stings with his double tongue insofar as his false words are hurtful. But what is metaphorically true of Demetrius is not, according to Johnson, actually true of adders, and, although he does not say so in his notes to Shakespeare, Johnson demands that both parts of a metaphor make sense for it to be justifiable.

Johnson expresses his objection in the *Life of Cowley* to "wit which consists of thoughts true in one sense of the expression, and false in the other". He argues, such "confusion of images may entertain for a moment, but being unnatural it soon grows wearisome".[3] And in *Idler* No. 34, Johnson reminds us that illustrations which "have more of genius but less of truth . . . often please, but they never convince".[4] Furthermore, it may be that Johnson's objection to metaphors of which the vehicles contain inaccuracies is based in part upon his belief that

. . . the force of metaphors is lost when the mind by the mention of particulars is turned more upon the original than the secondary sense, more upon that from which the illustration is drawn than that to which it is applied.[5]

As we see so clearly from Johnson's own critical analyses, an inaccurate vehicle calls attention – at least Johnson's attention – to itself and away from that which it is supposed to illustrate. If the purpose of a metaphor is illustration, then it must be not only clear, but true.[6]

Johnson made the same demand of simile. He objected to the following lines from Cowley's "The Heartbreaking" because the simile of the concluding line is literally false:

It gave a piteous groan, and so it broke;
In vain it something would have spoke:
The love within too strong for 't was,
Like poison put into a Venice-glass.[7]

[3] *Lives*, I, 41.
[4] *Idler and Adventurer*, p. 107 .
[5] "Life of Cowley", *Lives*, I, 45.
[6] We may, of course, cite as additional evidence of Johnson's position his general remark, "the basis of all excellence is truth". (*Lives*, I, 6.)
[7] Quoted by Johnson in "Life of Cowley", *Lives*, I, 33.

Love may break a heart, but poison will NOT break a Venice-glass.
Of the Metaphysical poets, Johnson therefore writes,

> They were not always strictly curious whether the opinions from which
> they drew their illustrations were true; it was enough that they were popu-
> lar. Bacon remarks, that some falsehoods are continued by tradition, because
> they supply commodious allusions.[8]

But to Johnson, an allusion proved false could not be commodious.
One cannot learn from false examples. Or rather, one might learn
the opposite of the lesson intended. He who knows that poison
does not break glasses may doubt that love breaks hearts.

Johnson's objection to the Metaphysical simile is not that it is
far-fetched. If a simile is far-fetched and yet apt, so much the better,
for a simile is not an exemplification. Johnson is careful to distinguish the two in his *Life of Addison*, where he gives his most tho-
rough definition of simile:

> A poetical simile is the discovery of likeness between two actions in their
> general nature dissimilar, or of causes terminating by different operations
> in some resemblance of effect. But the mention of another like consequence
> from a like cause, or of a like performance by a like agency, is not a simile,
> but an exemplification. It is not a simile to say that the Thames waters
> fields as the Po waters fields; or that as Hecla vomits flames in Iceland,
> so Aetna vomits flames in Sicily.[9]

Also, in the *Life of Pope*, Johnson complains,

> In their similes the greatest writers have sometimes failed: the ship-race,
> compared with the chariot race, is neither illustrated nor aggrandised;
> land and water make all the difference: when Apollo, running after Daphne
> is likened to a greyhound chasing a hare, there is nothing gained; the ideas
> of pursuit and flight are too plain to be made plainer . . .[10]

And again, in the *Life of Dryden*, Johnson objects to a simile
because "there is so much likeness in the initial comparison that
there is no illustration".[11] Such similes are not similes at all, nor is
illustration illustration when ideas are 'too plain to be made
plainer'. For a simile to succeed, it must accomplish what exempli-

---

[8] "Life of Cowley", *Lives*, I, 33.
[9] *Lives*, II, 129—130.
[10] *Lives*, III, 230.
[11] *Lives*, I, 441.

fication cannot. Johnson gives his rule of excellence in a simile
of his own:

A simile may be compared to lines converging at a point and is more excellent as the lines approach from greater distance: an exemplification may be
considered as two parallel lines which run on together without approxima-
tion, never far separated, and never joined.[12]

Johnson's displeasure, then, with Cowley's simile of the Venice-
glass and others like it is not that the lines approach from too great
a distance, but that they do not converge.

Johnson – Dictionary Johnson – in no way confuses the concepts
of simile, metaphor, and allegory. If his definitions are not exact
enough for the purposes of modern criticism, we must remember
that he composed them for a dictionary of the English language,
not a handbook of literary terms. Nevertheless, he manages to
keep the three terms distinct while pointing to their common
nature: all three consist of analogy. For Johnson, it is the propriety
of the analogy that determines the excellence of each. Johnson
judges allegory, metaphor, and simile by the same standard, and
when he condemns examples of them, it is for the same faults.

Of the three, allegory is the most likely to contain flaws because
of its usually greater length. In the *Dictionary*, Johnson quotes
Ben Jonson's admonition, "Neither must we draw out our *allegory*
too long, lest either we make ourselves obscure, or fall into affectation, which is childish." Johnson, if not Jonson, no doubt meant
us to equate affectation with the use of allusions which are commodious although false, thereby giving authority to his demand
that allegory, like metaphor and simile, exhibit not only clarity
but truth. The requirements of truth and clarity are almost separable and correspond to the two sides of the analogy which is
presented. The literal or pictorial meaning (vehicle) must be free
of contradiction or falsehood; the metaphorical or abstract meaning
(tenor) must avoid obscurity.

When Johnson complains of Milton's "Lycidas" that Milton and
Edward King "never drove a field, and that they had no flocks
to batten",[13] he is complaining of obscurity:

... though it be allowed that the representation may be allegorical, the

---

[12] "Life of Addison", *Lives*, II, 130.
[13] *Lives*, I, 164.

true meaning is so uncertain and remote that it is never sought because it cannot be known when it is found.[14]

Shepherds do drive their flocks in the field; the literal side of the analogy is true enough. But Johnson finds the metaphorical meaning impossible to determine and therefore rejects the basic analogy as useless. When, on the other hand, Johnson writes of Dryden's *Absalom and Achitophel,*

The original structure of the poem was defective: allegories drawn to great length will always break; Charles could not run continually parallel with David,[15]

it is not obscurity that he complains of; the metaphorical meaning of the poem had been clear to everyone. The trouble is that the actions of the poem are truer of Charles than of David. On the literal level the parallel does not hold. King David had no brother who was a legitimate heir to the throne, yet Absalom mentions such a brother. The reference to James is clear, but the analogy is false. The allegory breaks on the literal level; it is clear but not true.

Johnson's word for lack of truth was 'absurdity'. He found no allegory more absurd than that in which allegorical persons are used to conduct actions. Twice in the Lives of the Poets – in the *Life of Pope* and in the *Life of Milton* – Johnson makes the same complaint against the allegory of abstract personification, and each time uses the word 'absurdity':

The employment of allegorical persons always excites conviction of its own absurdity: they may produce effects, but cannot conduct actions; when the phantom is put in motion, it dissolves; thus Discord may raise a mutiny, but Discord cannot conduct a march, nor besiege a town.[16]

To exalt causes into agents, to invest abstract ideas with form, and animate them with activity has always been the right of poetry. But such airy beings are for the most part suffered only to do their natural office, and retire. Thus Fame tells a tale and Victory hovers over a general or perches on a standard; but Fame and Victory can do no more. To give them any real employment or ascribe to them any material agency is to make them allegorical no longer, but to shock the mind by ascribing effects to non-entity. In the *Prometheus* of Aeschylus we see Violence and Strength, and in the

[14] *Lives,* I, 164.
[15] *Lives,* I, 436—437.
[16] *Lives,* III, 233.

Alcestis of Euripides we see Death, brought upon the stage, all as active persons of the drama; but no precedents can justify absurdity.[17]

There are two kinds of abstract personification, and Johnson finds one of them absurd. Bertrand Bronson, in his reconsideration of personification, calls the two kinds restrictive and non-restrictive.[18] According to Professor Bronson's classification, the non-restrictive figure characterizes within the normal field of the concept, and the restrictive characterizes outside that field. To use Johnson's examples, Fame telling a tale or Victory perching on a standard is non-restrictive; Discord conducting a march or besieging a town is restrictive. Johnson found the restrictive absurd and in his own writings generally made use only of the non-restrictive figure. But Bronson points out that to modern readers, the non-restrictive abstract personification is the most likely to give offense, and considers it responsible for most modern students' difficulty in enjoying Johnson's own poem, "On the Death of Dr. Robert Levet".

Non-restrictive does not mean non-distinct. Fame can do no more than what is within the normal field of the concept, but what is within the normal field of the concept only Fame can do. Victory cannot tell a tale. Indistinct personification is itself absurd, and Johnson condemned it where he found it. He says of a stanza of Gray's "The Bard",

The personification is indistinct. Thirst and Hunger are not alike, and their features, to make the imagery perfect, should have been discriminated.[19]

It is not enough that Thirst and Hunger conduct no actions; their effects must be distinguished for the personification to be just. To confuse the two defeats the purpose. Personification requires individualization. One is tempted to say characterization. The personified abstraction must not step out of character, and no two abstractions may be given the same character unless the abstract concepts themselves are synonymous.

If in the foregoing few pages I have placed greater emphasis upon Johnson's demand for truth than upon his demand for clarity,

[17] *Lives,* I, 185.
[18] Bertrand H. Bronson, "Personification Reconsidered", in *New Light On Dr. Johnson,* ed. Frederick W. Hilles (New Haven, Yale University Press, 1959), pp. 200ff.
[19] *Lives,* III, 440.

I have done so because in demanding clarity, Johnson was doing no more than reiterating the eighteenth-century preference for allegory which exhibited classical simplicity as opposed to the 'dark-veiled' allegory of the Renaissance and Middle Ages.[20] In his demand for truth Johnson stands out among his contemporaries.

The type of allegory which early in the century Addison introduced – or, as he felt, revived – was, according to Johnson's standards, clear, simple, and absurd. In the *Guardian* of September 4, 1713, Addison credits himself with having "revived several antiquated ways of writing" and mentions particularly "those allegories, wherein virtues, vices, and human passions, are introduced as real actors".[21] These remarks serve to introduce an allegory by Addison in which Patience commands an army. It is true that Patience is not so soon tired out as the opposing general – she "had been repulsed above a hundred times, and rallied as often"[22] until her enemy was ready to yield – but it is surely not within the normal field of the concept of Patience to have her conduct an offense or rally so often. To give Patience such real employment is not only "to shock the mind by ascribing effects to non-entity",[23] but to shock the mind by ascribing effects to the WRONG non-entity. Had Perseverance or Strategy won the battle we should not have been disturbed, but having Patience win the battle by losing her character is silly as well as self-defeating.

Yet Addison's allegories did not appear absurd to his contemporaries. We have only to read John Hughes's essay of 1715, "On Allegorical Poetry", to understand why. Hughes allows to the writer of allegories liberties which he would allow to no other writer:

. . . Allegory has a liberty indulg'd to it beyond any other sort of Writing whatsoever; . . . it often assembles things of the most contrary kinds in

---

[20] Mr. Edwin C. Heinle in his study "The Eighteenth-Century Allegorical Essay" (Columbia University dissertation, 1957) points out that eighteenth-century allegorists "believed they were reviving allegory in its ancient form, avoiding the ambiguity of the Middle Ages and the Renaissance, and returning to the purer models of the Greeks". He adds that "two short works in particular, the *Choice of Hercules* and the *Table of Cebes*, were considered the perfect models because of their clarity and simplicity". (p. iii.)

[21] Addison, *Guardian* No. 152, *Works*, ed. Richard Hurd (London, 1811), V, 322.

[22] Addison, *Works*, V, 324.

[23] "Life of Milton", *Lives*, I, 185.

Nature, and supposes even Impossibilities; . . . and it abounds in such Licenses as wou'd be shocking and monstrous, if the Mind did not attend to the mystick Sense contain'd under them.[24]

Hughes, it is true, distinguishes two kinds of allegory, one of which consists of "real or historical Persons, and probable or possible Actions; by which however some other Persons and Actions are typify'd or represented",[25] but he feels such allegory hardly deserves the name and makes it clear that another kind of allegory is his main concern:

> The second kind of Allegory, and which, I think, may more properly challenge the Name, is that in which the Fable or Story consists for the most part of fictitious Persons or Beings, Creatures of the Poet's Brain, and Actions surprising, and without the Bounds of Probability or Nature. In Works of this kind, it is impossible for the Reader to rest in the literal Sense, but he is of necessity driven to seek for another Meaning under these wild Types and Shadows. This Grotesque Invention claims, as I have observ'd, a Licence peculiar to it self, and is what I wou'd be understood in this Discourse more particularly to mean by the word Allegory.[26]

To Hughes, then, improbability was a part of allegory almost by definition. The literal sense might be nonsense so long as it contained a 'mystick' sense under it which could be easily discerned. Alexander Pope expresses the identical view in a note to his *Temple of Fame*, which appeared in the same year as Hughes's essay. Pope speaks of "this visionary and allegorical kind of Poetry, which admits of every Wild Object that Fancy may present in a Dream, and where it is sufficient if the moral Meaning atone for the Improbability".[27] It is no wonder that the literal sense was so often presented by eighteenth-century allegorists as a dream or vision; we do not expect dreams to make literal sense although we desire clear interpretations of them. Johnson employed the dream framework in his own allegories far less than did his contemporaries.

It is apparent from a pair of parallel passages that Johnson read Hughes's essay and that it stayed in his mind. When in his *Life*

---

[24] John Hughes, "On Allegorical Poetry", in *Critical Essays of the Eighteenth Century 1700—1715*, ed. Willard Higley Durham (New Haven, Yale University Press, 1915; New York, Russell & Russell, 1961), pp. 90—91.

[25] Hughes, p. 91.

[26] Hughes, p. 92.

[27] Note to *Temple of Fame*, ll. 53—60, in Alexander Pope, *Twickenham Edition of the Poems*, Vol. II: *The Rape of the Lock and Other Poems*, ed. Geoffrey Tillotson, 3rd ed. (London, Methuen & Co., 1962), p. 410.

of Milton, Johnson, in the passage which I had occasion to refer to earlier, wrote,

In the *Prometheus* of Aeschylus we see Violence and Strength, and in the *Alcestis* of Euripides we see Death, brought upon the stage, all as active persons of the drama; but no precedents can justify absurdity,[28]

he was either unconsciously or consciously answering the following passage from Hughes's essay:

Thus in a Tragedy of *Aeschylus*, *Strength* is introduc'd assisting *Vulcan* to bind *Prometheus* to a Rock; and in one of *Euripides*, *Death* comes to the House of *Admetus* to demand *Alcestis*, who had offer'd her self to die to save her Husband's Life. But what I have here said of Epick and Dramatick Poems does not extend to such Writings, the very Frame and Model of which is design'd to be Allegorical; in which therefore, as I said before, such unsubstantial and symbolical Actors may be very properly admitted.[29]

Hughes approves no more than Johnson of having allegorical figures brought upon the stage as active persons of the drama, but he allows the liberty of employing such actors to the writer of allegories. Johnson, in the passage in the *Life of Milton*, simply extends Hughes's prohibition to all writing. To Johnson, what is absurd in one medium will be absurd in another and that is the end of it. The idea of Patience conducting an army is absurd and we do not have to see it on a stage to realize it. Hughes, on the other hand, felt that the reader did not stay with the literal sense of an allegory long enough to picture it; the reader jumps to the 'mystick' sense and the problem of absurdity is avoided. Hughes was therefore able to consider the allegories of Addison examples of 'the Perfection to which this kind of Writing is capable of being rais'd'.[30]

Hughes should not be misunderstood, although he most likely was misunderstood by eighteenth-century allegorists who took more liberties with their fables than even Hughes meant to allow. The four qualities which Hughes lists as essential to every good allegory are qualities which Johnson also insisted upon. If anything, Johnson interpreted Hughes's rules more strictly than Hughes himself did. Hughes requires: (1) that the fable or literal sense "be lively, and surprizing", (2) "Aptness in the Fable to the Subject on

[28] *Lives*, I, 185.
[29] Hughes, pp. 96—97.
[30] Hughes, p. 104.

which it is employ'd", (3) "that the Fable be every where consistent with it self", and (4) "that the Allegory be clear and intelligible".[31] The first and fourth of these rules Johnson would accept without qualification; it is in his application of the second and third requirements that he differs from Hughes. According to Johnson, a fable cannot be appropriate to a subject if the fable is untrue. His criticism of the 'commodious allusions' of the Metaphysical Poets applies to allegories as well. An illustration cannot be commodious if it is false. Similarly, a fable cannot be consistent with itself if the fable is absurd. By absurdity, Johnson often means no more than inconsistency. In the *Dictionary*, he defines absurd when used of practices rather than persons as 'inconsistent, contrary to reason'. For Patience to conduct a battle is absurd because aggression is not consistent with the concept of patience. A fable in which Patience is so employed can therefore not be "every where consistent with it self". Hughes created sound rules for good allegory and then granted allegorists the liberty of breaking them. Johnson was not so liberal.

Johnson's demand for consistency might be looked upon as a recognition of the validity of the principle of decorum when it is applied sensibly. Johnson believed "rules are the instruments of mental vision, which may, indeed, assist our faculties when properly used, but produce confusion and obscurity by unskilful application".[32] To be sure, Johnson found nothing wrong with depicting a senator of Rome as a buffoon, but that, he tells us, is because buffoons may be found in senate-houses as readily as elsewhere.[33] When Johnson criticizes Dennis and Rymer and Voltaire, it is not the principle of decorum but the "petty cavils of petty minds" that he condemns. Decorum indeed demands that we place at least one buffoon in any senate-house, and Shakespeare does not violate it. Johnson's displeasure with the abstract personifications of other allegorists is due precisely to their failure to maintain decorum. Fame may do no more than tell a tale because to do more would be inappropriate and out of character. Senators may engage in actions which make them look ridiculous and still be senators; abstract beings cannot engage in inappropriate actions and still

---

[31] Hughes, pp. 99—100.
[32] *Rambler* No. 176, *Works*, III, 328.
[33] "Preface to Shakespeare", *Works*, V, 109.

be abstract. If Johnson chose not to pay formal tribute to the principle of decorum, he did so only because he saw no need to invoke
an abused principle to condemn what reason alone could tell him
was absurd.

Johnson's allegories are not absurd. We shall see that they keep
closely to Johnson's own rules, which explains precisely why to
some commentators, they have seemed, in comparison with other
allegories of the period, to be lifeless and unpicturesque. Chester
F. Chapin, significantly, divides the personifications he finds in
works of the period into two types, one of which he calls allegorical
and the other metaphorical.[34] He claims that Johnson's personifications are metaphorical whereas those of Collins and Gray are
allegorical, although he admits that no sharp line may be drawn
between the two types. Chapin's division is similar to Bronson's
distinction between restrictive and non-restrictive personifications,
but his use of the term metaphorical for what Bronson would call
non-restrictive is revealing, if inaccurate. According to Chapin,
Johnson's personified abstractions have "the virtues of metaphor"
rather than "the virtues of the allegorical picture".[35] And the virtue
of metaphor, he tells us, is "a close and significant interaction
between image and idea".[36] Johnson considered such interaction,
or, as he put it, convergence, no more a virtue of metaphor than of
simile or allegory. Chapin perhaps confuses allegory and allegorical
picture. But what Chapin has noticed is that Johnson's personifications, because they are non-restrictive, are not especially picturesque and that therein lies their virtue. An image must be transparent
enough for an idea to shine through. Johnson's insistence upon
propriety of analogy, whether in a simile, metaphor, or allegory,
causes his abstractions to resemble less figures of tapestry than
figures of rhetoric.

[34] Chester F. Chapin, *Personification in Eighteenth-Century English Poetry*
(New York, King's Crown Press, 1955), p. 3.
[35] Chapin, p. 105.
[36] Chapin, p. 114.

IV

THE ALLEGORICAL PUN

I would be better pleased if the English language permitted me to speak in the present chapter of 'punical' allegory instead of allegorical pun. For it is not my intention here to create new categories for classifying puns (the two very sensible and already existing categories of good and bad, which I shall have occasion to use later on, will serve my purpose more than adequately). The allegorical pun is in fact a completely ordinary type of pun (except that it is never bad) but a very special and distinctly Johnsonian type of allegory. The aim of this chapter is to call attention to the large number of Johnson's allegorical metaphors which are also good puns and to show the effect of such puns on the nature of his allegory.

Something must first be said of Johnson's "general aversion to a pun", which Boswell so persistently asserts.[1] It is quite likely that Johnson, and there is no doubt that Boswell, both under the influence of Addison's condemnation of puns in one of his several essays on true and false wit,[2] generally considered punning a low form of wit. Surely Johnson has not often been thought of as a punster. Nevertheless Boswell does present several instances in his *Life of Johnson* of his idol's appreciation and admiration of good puns,[3] and, however reluctantly, does on occasion allow us to hear Johnson indulging in the making of a good-humored pun himself.[4] Moreover William Empson, whose influence is largely responsible for whatever gains in respectability the pun has made in our own day, includes two puns from Johnson's two most famous poems

[1] *Life*, IV, 316; II, 241.
[2] *Spectator* No. 61.
[3] *Life*, II, 241; III, 322–323; IV, 316.
[4] *Life*, III, 232, 325; IV, 73, 99.

among the four examples of eighteenth-century puns with which he illustrates his third type of ambiguity.[5]

Let us then see if we cannot determine what kind of pun Johnson and his near-contemporaries objected to and what kind they admired. And here we may do well to use the aforementioned categories of good and bad. Addison, to be sure, seems to condemn all puns whatever, but not without giving a specific reason, and not without granting that "the seeds of punning are in the minds of all men".[6] Addison's reason for objecting to puns is that he considers any pun "a sound, and nothing but a sound". His test for a piece of wit is to translate it into a different language: "if it bears the test you may pronounce it true; but if it vanishes in the experiment you may conclude it to have been a pun".[7] But while we must agree with Addison that a pun will not often remain a pun when trans-

---

[5] The puns which Empson points to involve the words *licensed* and *will* in the two following passages:

> Let such raise palaces, and manors buy,
> Collect a tax, or farm a lottery,
> With warbling eunichs fill a *licens'd* stage,
> And lull to servitude a thoughtless age.
>
> *(London, ll. 57—60.)*

> The watchful guests still hint the last offence,
> The daughter's petulance, the son's expence,
> Improve his heady rage with treach'rous skill,
> And mould his passions till they make his *will*.
>
> *(The Vanity of Human Wishes, ll. 279—282.)*

Of the first passage, Empson writes, "*Licensed* refers, I understand, to the passing of the Licensing Act, and adds with a peculiarly energetic sneer that they had all kinds of goings-on. This, I take it, is a joke; one would say it with an accent on *licensed* and look knowingly at the listener to make sure he saw the point." Empson refers to the word *will* in the second passage as 'a careful, very conscious pun' and calls our attention to still another pun in the line above: "Consider the word *heady*, which means both that he was head of the family and that his passions soon came to a head; it is the same sort of pun as the conscious one about the *will*, and yet one can absorb it without recognising it at all." *(Seven Types of Ambiguity,* 2nd ed., London, Chatto & Windus, 1947, pp. 107—108.)

[6] *The Spectator,* ed. George A. Aitken (London, George Routledge & Sons, Ltd.), I, 259.

[7] *Spectator* (No. 61), I, 263.

lated into another language, we shall see that the wit of a good pun is not based on sound alone.[8]

We may define a pun as the occurrence of a word-sound in such an environment that two different meanings, whether of the same word or of different words with the same sound, strike the ear simultaneously. The truth or falsehood of a pun's wit depends upon whether both or only one of the meanings is logically relevant in the context. A bad pun contains a logically irrelevant meaning. Unless both meanings in a pun make equally good sense, its wit will not only fail to survive translation into another language; it will vanish under even the slightest amount of examination in its own language. An example of a bad pun should make my meaning clear. I quote an irresistible one which Professor Wimsatt happens to include in the introduction to his anthology of Alexander Pope's poetry:

Why is a dog more warmly clad in summer than in winter? Because in winter he wears a fur coat; but in summer he wears a fur coat and pants.[9]

Such a pun makes one groan, and it deserves no better reception. Its supposed wit vanishes the instant it is grasped. "Wears pants" has no meaning in the sentence; it only sounds as if it has meaning. What Addison says is in fact true of bad puns: they consist of "a sound and nothing but a sound".

Good puns consist of a coincidence of sound and meaning. Two different meanings that happen to sound the same are both meant. The purer but rarer form of good pun is that in which the different meanings of two etymologically unrelated homonyms are made relevant i n a single context, as in Shakespeare's sonnet beginning

[8] Addison's remarks are perhaps more indicative of a new seriousness with which puns were taken in the eighteenth century than of a general distaste for punning. According to William Empson, the Elizabethans "would treat puns as mere casual bricks, requiring no great refinement, of which any number could easily be collected for a flirtation or indignant harangue", whereas by the eighteenth century "the great thing about a pun was that it was not a Bad Pun, that it satisfied the Unities and what not; it could stand alone and would expect admiration, and was a much more elegant affair". (Empson, p. 66.) The new attitude may be related to the more general objections of Dryden and Pope toward any instances in poetry of sound without sense.

[9] William K. Wimsatt, Jr., ed., Pope, *Selected Poetry and Prose* (New York, Rinehart & Co., 1951), p. xxxii, n. 1.

"When my love swears that she is made of truth", where the verb meaning 'to tell an untruth' and the verb meaning 'to recline' are equally well-suited to the context each time the word-sound 'lie' occurs. But languages provide few homonyms like lie and lie. The more common type of pun plays upon two meanings of the same word, as for example the Duchess's pun in *Alice in Wonderland*, "flamingos and mustard both bite".[10] Here the same word is used both in a literal and a metaphorical sense. It is the sort of statement that Johnson would have objected to if a Metaphysical poet offered it as a proof of the similarity of flamingos and mustard. But as a piece of wit, it is no less 'true' than Pope's famous line, "Or stain her honour or her new brocade", which one cannot imagine either Johnson or Addison objecting to.[11]

"Metaphor or pun or both?", asks Professor Wimsatt about the word 'stain' in Pope's excellent line.[12] 'Both' would seem to be the only satisfactory answer, but it is an answer that gives rise to new questions. Certainly not all metaphors are puns. When is a metaphor a pun? What is it about Pope's metaphor that makes it also a good pun? Is it simply the expert structure of the line? I think not. There would be no pun if the line were "Or *tear* her honour or her new brocade". When, then, is a metaphor a pun? Only when it is a dead metaphor that has been brought to life. Only when the metaphorical use of the word is common in ordinary speech. Because we are so used to hearing one speak of a stain upon one's honor or

[10] Chapter IX.

[11] Perhaps when Johnson, in his *Dictionary*, defined the word *quibble* as "A low conceit depending on the sound of words; a pun", he meant to indicate that quibbles depend ONLY on the sound of words and not the meaning. Johnson's famous objection to Shakespeare's 'quibbles' would then be that they are often BAD puns. Indeed Johnson states that Shakespeare's quibbles are produced at "the sacrifice of reason, propriety and truth". (*Works*, V, 118.) Presumably Johnson had no objection to puns which do not sacrifice reason, propriety, and truth.

The other major instance in which Johnson's 'aversion to a pun' might seem to show itself, involves his remarks concerning the conversation of Edmund Burke, who was an avid punster. Boswell records the following statement by Johnson on the subject of Burke's verbal wit: " 'Tis low; 'tis conceit. I used to say, Burke never once made a good joke." (*Journal of a Tour to the Hebrides*, ed. L. F. Powell, London, J. M. Dent & Sons, Ltd., 1958, p. 13.) But here too it may be that Johnson felt Burke too often sacrificed meaning for sound.

[12] Introduction to Pope, *Selected Poetry and Prose*, p. xxx.

good name or reputation that we are apt to forget it is a metaphor, we are able to hear Pope's line as a pun on two homonyms when the dead metaphor's literal meaning is suddenly restored. In other words, puns of the type that play upon two different meanings of the same word strike the ear in the same way that puns which make use of genuine homonyms do. Otherwise they would not be recognized as puns.

Do I mean to say that the enlivening of a dead metaphor invariably produces a pun? I do. When a metaphor that is dead or almost dead in common use is placed in a context where its literal meaning becomes relevant, the result is necessarily a pun.

Samuel Johnson's practice of enlivening dead metaphors has long been noted as a distinctive feature of his prose style. William Wimsatt, in *The Prose Style of Samuel Johnson*, points to his "tendency to reverse dead metaphors, to force them back to their etymological meaning so that they assume a new metaphorical life" as "the thing most characteristic" of Johnson's imagery.[13] And, again, in *Philosophic Words*, Professor Wimsatt notes that Johnson's "realization of the imagery latent in even the most abstract philosophic word is so keen, that a very accurate degree of metaphoric interaction between abstract and ordinarily almost imageless words often occurs in his writing".[14]

The famous example that comes to mind, Johnson's use of the word *ardour* in its etymological sense of 'burning heat', was noted as long ago as 1786 by the Reverend Robert Burrowes in his "Essay on the Stile of Doctor Samuel Johnson":

Thus *ardour*, which in his preface to his Dictionary, he observes, is never used to denote material heat, yet to an etymologist would naturally suggest it; and Johnson accordingly, speaking of the "*ardour* of posthumous fame", says that "some have considered it as little better than *splendid* madness; as a *flame kindled* by pride and *fanned* by folly".[15]

By placing the word *ardour* in the proper environment, Johnson

---

[13] W. K Wimsatt, Jr., *The Prose Style of Samuel Johnson* (New Haven, Yale University Press, 1941), p. 66.

[14] W. K. Wimsatt, Jr., *Philosophic Words* (New Haven, Yale University Press, 1948) p. 66.

[15] Robert Burrowes, "Essay on the Stile of Doctor Samuel Johnson", No. II (November 13, 1786), *The Transactions of the Royal Irish Academy* (Dublin, 1787), p. 49. Also cited by Wimsatt, *Prose Style*, p. 66.

turns an "ordinarily almost imageless word" into a lively metaphor.

Or, to take an example that has, to my knowledge, not been commented upon before, consider the verb 'to insult' in the following sentence from Johnson's *Rambler* No. 12:

Insulted ! Get down stairs, you slut, or the footman shall *insult* you.[16]

If we grant that in its modern use the word 'insult' is a metaphor, it is certainly a dead one. Hardly anyone stops to think of it as a metaphor at all. But Johnson did. He knew that it was derived from the Latin verb *insultare*, meaning "to leap at or on", and in his *Dictionary* he gives "to trample upon; to triumph over" as an English meaning of the word. Johnson's supporting illustrations from *King Lear*, Dryden, and Dryden's Virgil unfortunately fail to establish that 'to trample upon' is ever meant literally. But the O. E. D. lists a possible example of such usage from Shaftesbury: "The sacred Pomp trodden under-foot, insulted."[17] And I am reminded of a better-known illustration, which the O. E. D. and Johnson both miss. In Shakespeare, Titus Andronicus, speaking of a dead fly, says, "Give me thy knife, I will insult on him" (III, ii, 71). meaning that he will beat it with his knife, which he does when he says the words a few lines below, "There's for thyself, and that's for Tamora" (III, ii, 74).

Now look again at Johnson's line,

Insulted! Get down stairs, you slut, or the footman shall *insult* you.

Johnson uses the word 'insulted' first in its ordinary dead-metaphorical sense and then, by repeating the verb in a slightly different context, restores it to its etymological meaning. In so doing, he creates a bilingual pun that the many of his contemporary readers who had been educated in Latin would not fail to catch.[18] And the

---

[16] *Works*, II, 60.

[17] The example is given as an illustration of the meaning 'to assail with offensively dishonouring or contemptuous speech or action'. The O. E. D. does not list 'to trample upon' among the meanings of insult, but it does recognize 'to attack, assault, assail' and 'to leap wantonly'.

[18] Perhaps even the word 'footman' in the same sentence becomes a pun: "Get down stairs, you slut, or the *foot*man shall [use his foot to] insult you." Furthermore, there is the possibility, suggested by the word 'slut', that 'insult' in its sense 'to leap on' refers here to the sex act.

examples from Shaftesbury and Shakespeare cited above give us good reason to believe that even Johnson's readers with no Latin could have recognized a pun on two different English meanings of the word 'insult', one common and metaphorical, the other less common and literal. We may find similar examples throughout all of Johnson's prose. But it is time to examine the specific effect that this general characteristic of Johnson's prose style has upon his allegory.

Those critics who have sought to determine the nature of allegory by examination of its effect upon the reader have accurately pointed out that there is in the normal operation of allegory what may be termed a 'time-lag'. Professor Ellen Douglass Leyburn describes it as "the brief interval in which the reader makes the adjustment between the apparent meaning and the real one".[19] The adjustment is supposedly in the nature of a translation from the only meaning the reader hears to the meaning he is finally to understand. The reader's first task is to discover the key or scale according to which the necessary conversions are to be made. Even where the allegorical figures are given obvious and transparent names, the reader must still translate what he hears from one context to another: the figure of Patience in the fable must be converted to the quality of patience in the mind. The allegorist is not usually capable of making himself heard in two contexts at the same time. If he should manage to do so, the result would be a pun. Samuel Johnson manages to do so.

Allegory gives Johnson muchg reater opportunity than ordinary prose to restore dead metaphors to life. For it is the function of allegory to present abstract concepts in concrete form. The allegorist is, of course, free to choose whatever concrete form he wishes. But since so much of abstract language consists of dead metaphor, why not, by enlivening the dead metaphor, present the abstract concept in the concrete form from which it originally sprang?

That is what Johnson commonly does. His allegorical metaphors

---

[19] Ellen Douglass Leyburn, *Satiric Allegory: Mirror of Man* (New Haven, Yale University Press, 1956), p. 10.

do not often startle us with the uniqueness of their conception. Their excellence lies, rather, in the success with which they restore vivid imagery to metaphors of common speech which have become worn out with use. And, perhaps contrary to normal expectation, the most worn-out metaphors are the ones that serve Johnson best. For, as we have seen in Johnson's non-allegorical prose, when a dead metaphor is revived a pun is produced.

The special importance of such puns in Johnson's allegories is that they enable him to avoid the 'time-lag' which the theorists tell us is part of the usual working of allegory. For when an allegorical metaphor is also a pun (resulting from the restoration of imagery to a common dead metaphor), there is no adjustment to be made between the apparent meaning (vehicle) and the real one (tenor) since the reader is already accustomed to hearing the real meaning expressed by the apparent one. If there is any time-lag in such a metaphor, it goes in just the opposite direction from 'the normal operation of allegory'. If the real meaning is not grasped at the same moment as the apparent meaning, it is grasped a moment before it – which is to say, of course, that the real meaning is, if anything, more apparent than the 'apparent' one, and we had better watch our terms.

Let us turn, then, to illustrations. I have chosen from Johnson's allegories four puns which are, I think, generally representative and yet different enough from one another to avoid needless repetition. I have said that all puns strike the ear in the same way or they would not be recognized as puns, but it must be admitted that some puns strike only the ears that are attuned to them. Some of Johnson's puns are obvious to any ear; others are such as only a lexicographer would make.

But fortunately the lexicographer has left us his *Dictionary*. Indeed there is nothing so convenient when you are trying to prove the presence of puns in an author's writing as having a dictionary by that author to refer to. If Johnson gives separate definitions with separate illustrations for the metaphorical and the literal use of a particular word, that is the best proof that by Johnson's time and to Johnson's mind the metaphorical use of the word had become too differentiated from the literal meaning to seem metaphorical any longer. Along with each of the four illustrations to be given below I shall therefore list both of the meanings from Johnson's *Dictionary* upon which the pun plays.

EXAMPLE 1.

... we had already passed the *straits* of infancy, in which multitudes had perished ...[20]

strait.

> a. A narrow pass, or frith.
> b. Distress; difficulty.

The quotations given in Johnson's *Dictionary* to illustrate the second meaning make it especially clear that in such an instance Johnson is not simply recording that a word is sometimes used as a metaphor but, rather, is showing us how a word has ceased to be a metaphor. For he seems purposely to have chosen such constructions as '*reduced to* streights' and '*under* any calamity or strait' in order to show that the metaphor has lost completely its original literal meaning.

In the present example from *Rambler* No. 102, literal meaning and vivid imagery are restored to the metaphor by making it a part of the allegory of the Ocean of Life. But the restoration of literal meaning does not result in the loss of figurative meaning. We hear both simultaneously and need not decide whether we are listening to an essay or a fable.

EXAMPLE 2.

... the vessels which had been shattered on the rocks of pleasure.[21]

vessel.

> a. Any vehicle in which men or goods are carried on the water.
> b. [In theology.] One relating to God's household.

The example is again from Johnson's allegory of the Ocean of Life, which easily provides a most appropriate context for the literal meaning of 'vessel'. The pun, though, is less obvious to a modern ear than the previous one on 'straits' because the metaphorical use of the word 'vessel' is no longer heard as frequently as it once was. But is was heard commonly enough in the sermons of Johnson's day, and the lengthy illustration in his *Dictionary* shows that the metaphor in such situations had become quite devoid of all imagery:

If the rigid doctrines be found apt to cool all those men's love of God, who have not the confidence to believe themselves of the number of the

[20] *Works*, II, 482.
[21] *Works*, II, 485.

few chosen *vessels*, and to beget security and presumption in others who
have conquered those difficulties. (Hammond)[22]

EXAMPLE 3.

. . . the wanderer may at length return after all his errours . . .[23]

errour.

>   a. Roving excursion; irregular course.
>   b. Mistake; involuntary deviation from truth.
>   c. [In theology.] Sin.

I have listed the literal meaning first because that is the order
Johnson follows in the *Dictionary*, but despite Johnson's supporting
illustration from Dryden, the usage has never been common in
English.[24] What we have, then, is a bilingual pun similar to the
one on 'insult' in *Rambler* No. 12. The Latin word *error* means
'a wandering', and in the context of Johnson's allegory of life as
the journey of a day (in *Rambler* No. 65) the Latin meaning is
entirely appropriate.[25] But surely to any English ear the metaphorical meaning, whether we take it to be 'mistakes' or 'sin', is the
one that is more immediately apparent. We therefore have a perfect example of time-lag in reverse, in which, if we are to use Miss
Leyburn's terms, the 'real' meaning is apparent and the 'apparent'
meaning is not apparent at all.

EXAMPLE 4.

. . . Minerva, therefore, deputed criticism to her [learning's] aid, who gener-
rally broke the *point* of satire's arrows, turned them aside, or retorted them
on himself.[26]

point.

>   a. The sharp end of any instrument, or body.
>   b. A sting of an epigram; a sentence terminated with some remarkable
>   turn of words or thought.

[22] *Dictionary*.

[23] *Works*, II, 313.

[24] Johnson explains his policy in his Preface: "the original sense of words
is often driven out of use by their metaphorical acceptations, yet must be
inserted for the sake of regular origination". (*Works*, V, 37.)

[25] Edmund Spenser earlier had played upon the Latin meaning of *error*
when he wrote, "This is the wandring wood, this *Errours* den." (*Faerie
Queene*, I, I, xiii.)

[26] *Works*, II, 112.

The example is from *Rambler* No. 22, which presents an allegorical battle between learning and wit. Satire shoots his arrows as the deputy of wit. The pun on the word 'point', clever and funny in itself, here does double duty. For the representation of what in everyday speech we might well refer to as 'the point of a satiric thrust' by the point of satire's arrows in an allegorical battle causes the word 'satire' itself to become something of a pun. As we hear both meanings of 'point' at the same time, so do we hear the word 'satire' referring at once to a figure in a fable and a species of wit.[27] There is no conversion to be made from one to the other: Johnson speaks in both contexts simultaneously.

The citation of four examples does not, of course, establish that there is a great frequency of puns in Johnson's allegory. And it may as well be admitted here that not all of Johnson's allegorical metaphors are puns. In the example cited above to show that the word 'vessel' was a pun, it might have been pointed out that the word 'rocks' was not one. 'Rocks of pleasure' is a metaphor neither dead nor appropriate, but we do not find many such in Johnson's allegories. In the allegory of the Ocean of Life, in which it occurs, it is far outweighed by the pun on 'vessel', which is repeated several times, and numerous other puns on 'launching', 'embarking', and 'sinking'. All counted, the puns occur frequently enough to keep our ears attuned to two different contexts at once throughout the entire allegory. So is it with almost any of Johnson's allegories that one may choose to examine.

To characterize Johnson's allegory in a word, it is not so much transparent as iridescent: we do not perceive a real context through an apparent one; rather, we perceive both together and observe their mutual interplay.

[27] As we shall see in the next chapter, another example in Johnson's allegory of a personified abstraction that is also a pun is the figure of Habit in "The Vision of Theodore", where Johnson continually puns upon dead-metaphorical phrases such as 'force of habit'.

V

"THE VISION OF THEODORE"

"The Vision of Theodore", which as the earliest of Johnson's allegorical pieces would be interesting to us in any event, is made even
more interesting by the fact that Johnson is known to have called
it "the best thing he ever wrote".[1] Unfortunately, Johnson's statement does not tell us quite as much as it appears to, for we do not
know exactly when it was made. Boswell, who had the remark se-
cond-hand from Bishop Percy, does not inform us when Johnson
uttered it or when Percy reported it. But the remark can be placed
within a period of four years. For Johnson first met Percy in 1756,
and the statement could have been made by Johnson no later than
March 12, 1760, on which date Percy related it in a letter to Shenstone.[2] Although we do not know whether or not Johnson had yet
written *Rasselas* (1759) when he called "The Vision of Theodore"
his best work, we can obtain some idea of how very highly he
thought of it if we recall that Johnson was already the author of
London and the *Life of Savage* when "The Vision of Theodore"
appeared in Dodsley's *Preceptor* in 1748 and that by 1756 Johnson
was known as the author of *The Vanity of Human Wishes, The
Rambler,* and the *Dictionary* as well.

"The Vision of Theodore" has received the scholarly attention of
Mr. Edwin C. Heinle in his "Eighteenth-Century Allegorical Essay",
a study which concentrates upon the history of identical allegorical
conventions in literature and art. Mr. Heinle finds Johnson's essay
unique in juxtaposing two allegorical mountains, each with a long
tradition of its own. The Mountain of Existence and the mountain-
which-affords-an-elevated-view-of-existence (Johnson's Mt. Tene-

---

[1] *Life,* I, 192.
[2] See *Life,* I, 537.

riffe) are equally conventional allegorical properties but, according to Mr. Heinle, they do not elsewhere occur together.[3]

I suppose that is a good thing to know. What is more interesting is to note that Johnson uses the convention of the mountain-which-affords-an-elevated-view-of-humanity in a delightfully unconventional way. Typically, one must climb to the highest summit of such a mountain in order to survey some prospect of humanity below. But Johnson's hermit has made hardly any progress toward the top of the mountain at the bottom of which he has lived for forty-eight years when, having already fallen asleep from laziness, he dreams that the following exchange takes place:

"Theodore, whither art thou going?" "I am climbing", answered I, "to the top of the mountain, to enjoy a more extensive prospect of the works of nature". "Attend first", (said he), "to the prospect which this place affords, and what thou dost not understand I will explain".[4]

This passage may be taken as a commentary on the corresponding portion of Addison's "Vision of Mirzah":

He then led me to the highest pinnacle of the rock, and placing me on the top of it, "Cast thy eyes eastward", said he, "and tell me what thou seest".[5]

Johnson's allegory by departing from the normal expectation of the familiar convention tells us clearly and forcefully that if we wish to survey human existence, all we need do is stand still and look about us. Johnson uses Mt. Teneriffe only to show that it is of no special use. To study humanity it is not, as other allegorists would have us believe, necessary to stand upon a lofty summit. "Deign on the passing world to turn thine eyes, / And pause a while from learning, to be wise."[6] Or, as his Protector actually puts it, when Theodore appears willing to look everywhere but in front of him, "the mountain of Existence is before thee, survey it, and be wise".[7]

---

[3] Edwin C. Heinle, "The Eighteenth-Century Allegorical Essay" (dissertation, Columbia University, 1957), p. 141. Mt. Teneriffe itself, a peak in the Canary Islands, was familiar to Johnson from Milton's *Paradise Lost* (IV, 987) and Donne's *First Anniversary* (286—288).

[4] *Works*, IX, 164.

[5] *The Spectator* (No. 159), ed. George A. Aitken (London, George Routledge & Sons, Ltd.), II, 230.

[6] "The Vanity of Human Wishes", *ll.* 157—158.

[7] *Works*, IX, 164.

The Mountain of Existence, although surely as public an allegorical property as any other, may also be looked upon as an expansion of a metaphor which comes naturally to Johnson whether he is writing allegory or not. The metaphor of human life, or some aspect of it, as a journey, particularly a steep, upward one, appears in Johnson's prose probably more frequently than any other image. One critic records more than a dozen separate occurrences of it – or rather, variations of it, for Johnson never repeats it identically – in *The Rambler* alone.[8]

But only in "The Vision of Theodore" does Johnson allow himself large enough scope to develop fully the possibilities of the metaphor of life's upward journey. No other allegorical image could possibly supply a more appropriate literal context for the majority of the dead metaphors that form so large a part of the traditional vocabulary of the language of practical morality. Such words as way, course, path, bypath; narrow, steep, rough, barren; rise, fall, climb, progress; lead, follow, direct, and guide all become recharged with imagery as they occur in the context of Theodore's vision. If in common speech the metaphorical usage of the word has not always become so differentiated from the literal meaning as to produce a pun, it is still in every case familiar enough to keep our attention functioning in two contexts at once without the aid of a key. When we hear Johnson's allegorical beings named in expressions such as 'path of Reason', 'followers of Religion', 'directions of Reason', not to mention 'force of Habit' and 'enchained by Habits', we are able to take them as literally or as figuratively as we may choose. But then we do not have to choose, for they can be taken entirely literally and entirely figuratively at the same time.

If in Johnson's allegory we need no key to move from one context to another, it is then necessary to ask what function is served by Theodore's Protector. For he would seem to be the traditional figure of the allegorical interpreter or guide, whose normal business is to explain what each of the figures in the fable stands for.

So far we have seen that Theodore's Protector serves the function of telling Theodore, whose eyes seem to be always in the wrong place, where to look if he wishes to see anything. Also, we may have

⁸ Cecil S. Emden, "Dr. Johnson And Imagery", *Review of English Studies*, New Series, Vol. I, No. 1 (1950), 31—32.

been reminded by certain of the Protector's words of statements similar in thought and even diction to those Johnson expresses elsewhere in his own person, so that we can regard the Protector as a spokesman for Johnson and compare his role in that respect to Imlac's in *Rasselas*. But at one point at least the Protector exercises a more peculiar function. Indeed his role becomes the exact opposite of that of the traditional interpreter: he serves to SUPPLY the imagery of the fable rather than explain it. Once again we may speak of time-lag in reverse. Only after Theodore has heard Education frequently cautioning those within her charge to beware of Habits does his Protector show him "a troop of pygmies, which appeared to walk silently before those that were climbing the mountain, and each to smooth the way before her follower".[9] In the normal operation of allegory the proper sequence would surely be first for Theodore to spy a troop of pygmies and then for his Protector to explain that they represent habits. By reversing the usual order Johnson does away completely with the possibility of any interval in which the fable might be apprehended before its allegory.

But Johnson has an even more important reason for having his Protector, rather than Theodore, notice the figures of Habit. For it is significant that Theodore should be unable to see the pygmies by himself. Habits are always likely to escape the notice of human beings, and Johnson never forgets that Theodore, unlike his Protector, is human. Theodore explains, "I found that I had missed the notice of them before, both because they were so minute as not easily to be discerned, and because they grew every moment nearer in their colour to the objects, with which they were surrounded."[10] Theodore's role is that of an observer, but he cannot be expected to observe without special aid what is normally missed by human observation. Even after he has discerned the presence of Habit and heard the repeated warnings of Education to her followers, Theodore confides, "Nor could I myself think her cautions so necessary as her frequent inculcation seemed to suppose . . .".[11] Theodore is no better able to perceive the dangers of Habit than any of the multitude who travel up the Mountain of Existence.

[9] *Works*, IX, 166.
[10] *Works*, IX, 166.
[11] *Works*, IX, 166.

Johnson takes care not to let his allegory become "a glass wherein beholders do generally discover everybody's face but their own".[12] Johnson is aware that the reader of an allegory will perforce place himself in the role of the observer; he therefore sees to it that his observer is in no way different from the multitude he observes.

The figure or figures of Habit – for Johnson lets Habit be singular or plural depending on which way it occurs in the particular phrase he happens to be making into an allegorical pun at the moment – are for any reader of "The Vision of Theodore" the center of attention. Indeed they are likely to call attention away from the basic structure of the Mountain of Existence. It may therefore be of some use simply to recount the plan of Johnson's allegorical mountain before proceeding further. The bottom of the Mountain, which is flowery and of gentle rise, is the province of Innocence, a mild governess, who continues her attendance but a little way before the travellers perceive themselves in the hands of Education, "a nymph more severe in her aspect, and imperious in her commands",[13] who confines them to certain paths which seem to them too narrow and too rough. Where the 'declivity' of the Mountain begins to grow craggy, Education resigns her charges to Reason and Religion, two powers of superior aspect, whose dominion extends to all the remaining part of the Mountain, although the prospect of Reason is terminated by a mist which is pierced only by the eyes of Religion. Beyond the mist are the Temples of Happiness, in which those who climb the precipice by the direction of Religion, "after the toil of their pilgrimage, repose for ever".[14] The numerous others, who, enticed by the calls of appetites and passions, forsake their guides at different stages in their journey up the Mountain, are led away to appropriate undesirable regions: the Caverns of Despair, the Bowers of Intemperance, the Maze of Indolence. Even those who leave the upward path only to retreat to the first part of the Mountain find upon returning there that they are no longer guarded by Innocence. (A return to the Happy Valley in *Rasselas*, we may assume, would be of a similar nature.)

[12] The words are from Swift's preface to *The Battle Of the Books*, where they refer specifically to satire and explain why "so very few are offended with it".

[13] *Works*, IX, 165.

[14] *Works*, IX, 169.

Such an account of the plan of Johnson's Mountain of Existence shows us something of the religious orthodoxy of his allegory, but little of its practical message and none of its color. If the figures of Habit captivate our attention at the expense of the larger structure of the allegory, that is as it should be, for the omnipresent threat of Habit is the heart of Johnson's message. The Mountain of Existence, it has been made clear, is a mountain of everyday existence that anyone may observe by looking about him. And whoever does but look about him will find nothing more apparent at every level of human existence than that man is a creature of habit. It is due to no lack of imagination on Johnson's part that at each stage (beyond the first) of his allegorical mountain one is confronted by the figure of Habit.

But the repetition indeed might have proved dull were not Johnson's figures of Habit the most entertaining of allegorical beings. For once we are apt to find ourselves being diverted by Johnson's allegory on the level of the fable alone, although the moral analogy is no less exact than elsewhere. The figures of Habit are as versatile a troop of performers as can be imagined. They are never dull because they are never the same. Their stature is "never at a stand but continually growing or decreasing, yet not always in the same proportions".[15] Sometimes we may see Habit "reduced to the stature of a dwarf, without strength and without activity", but then she will "on a sudden start into size".[16] On occasion, we may even see Habits making narrow roads easier and smoother, for Habits are not all bad; nor does Johnson suggest that men could do without them. But for the most part we see Habit doing her mischief: seizing victims in the Regions of Desire, dragging them to the Caverns of Despair, captivating the votaries of Religion, and seizing the followers of Reason while enlarging her size and doubling her chains "without intermission, and without reserve".[17]

The intense, not to say violent, activity which is ascribed to Habit might well cause a reader to ask whether Johnson in this case has not violated the rule he set forth in the *Life of Pope*, that allegorical beings "may produce effects, but cannot conduct actions".[18] Johnson, in his other allegories, and elsewhere in "The

[15] *Works*, IX, 166.
[16] *Works*, IX, 171.
[17] *Works*, IX, 173.
[18] *Lives*, III, 233.

Vision of Theodore", is especially careful not to let himself be found guilty of ascribing 'real employment' or 'material agency' to his personifications. He has them, for the most part, engage only in such 'actions' as conducting, counseling, cautioning, summoning, persuading, and enticing. In "The Vision of Theodore", appetites and passions may call to one side or the other. Religion can hold out her hand or recall her votaries by her emissary Conscience. But to seize, to drag, to enchain, are clearly beyond their power. The words which Johnson ascribes to the figure of Reason – "My power . . . is to advise, not to compel"[19] – while especially appropriate to the character of human reason, point to what Johnson considers a general qualification of the power of abstract beings. For we know that Johnson considered it absurd to allow activity to immateriality.

Yet the actions of Habit do not seem absurd for a number of reasons. For one thing, Johnson, in most instances, describes the actions of Habit in the passive voice: Theodore is shown 'Captives' who have been, or who are being, 'seized by Habits', 'enchained by Habits', 'withheld by Habit', 'led away by Habit'. The avoidance of the active voice transfers the emphasis from the actions of Habit to the effects of Habit upon her victims, in accordance with the Johnsonian rule ("allegorical persons . . . may produce effects, but cannot conduct actions"). Furthermore, the actions of Habit are not absurd because the phenomenon of habit, however abstractly considered, is a tangible one. We can speak not only of 'force of habit' but even of BREAKING a habit. Few other abstractions could have served Johnson so well.

Although there is no necessity to assume a particular model or source for "The Vision of Theodore", one classical allegory, the *Table* (Greek title: *Pinax*) of Cebes, deserves at least to be mentioned in this connection. Cebes' work was one of two short allegories that appeared with "The Vision of Theodore", in Part XII, the section entitled, "On Human Life and Manners", of Robert Dodsley's *Preceptor*, a two-volume survey of knowledge, designed for the self-education of the young, published in 1748, with a Preface by Samuel Johnson. Johnson describes Cebes' allegory in his Preface as a fable "of the highest Authority in the ancient *Pagan*

---

[19] *Works*, IX, 168.

World".[20] Actually, the work belongs to the first century, but it was long thought to have been written by the Cebes mentioned in Plato's Dialogues, who was a pupil of Socrates. Translated into English by John Healey in 1616, the short allegory formed part of a pocket-sized volume including the Characters of Theophrastus and the *Manual* of Epictetus, which went through several editions in the seventeenth century. Johnson was familiar with Cebes' work at least as early as 1735, when, in a letter to a young man, Samuel Ford, who apparently had asked Johnson for a list of books to study before entering a university, he listed Cebes first – perhaps mainly because of the easiness of his language – among the Greek authors he recommended.[21] It is certainly possible that Dodsley included Cebes' *Table* in *The Preceptor* on Johnson's recommendation.[22]

Cebes' allegory had also been praised by Addison. When Addison spoke of having revived the classical allegory practiced by the ancients, he had Cebes chiefly in mind. In *Tatler* No. 161, he introduces his allegory by declaring that he had been reading "that ancient and beautiful allegory, called 'The table of Cebes' '", when he had a dream which, he says, "I impute in some measure to the foregoing author, who has made an impression upon my imagination, and put me into his own way of thinking".[23] However that may be, the allegory which follows bears so little resemblance to the allegory of Cebes that Addison's early editor found it necessary to add this note:

> *The table of Cebes.*] A fine moral allegory, but of a character wholly different from that which follows. This picturesque and sublime dream had been more naturally introduced, if the author of it had fallen asleep over a *canto of Spenser*.[24]

Johnson's "Vision of Theodore", if not actually modelled after Cebes' *Table*, is at least more Cebesian than Spenserian. Although

---

[20] *The Preceptor*, 5th ed. (London, 1769), p. xxx. (Also *Works*, V, 245.)

[21] *The Letters of Samuel Johnson*, ed. R. W. Chapman (Oxford, Clarendon Press, 1952), I, 7.

[22] The version of Cebes' *Table* in *The Preceptor*, "translated into *English*, by a Person considerably distinguished in the Republic of Letters", was done by Joseph Spence.

[23] Addison, *Works*, ed. Richard Hurd (London, 1811), II, 368.

[24] Richard Hurd, ed., Addison, *Works*, II, 368.

Cebes uses the technique of ecphrasis rather than the framework of a dream-vision, his basic allegorical figure of a craggy hill which one must ascend along the path of true instruction in order to reach the habitation of Beatitude very definitely suggests Johnson's Mountain of Existence.[25] Furthermore, there is, significantly, the single mention in Cebes' allegory of 'the whole *Lernean* fen of vicious habits', which he who is crowned by Beatitude at last commands, 'whereas before they commaunded him'.[26] Cebes does not come near to assigning Habit the major role it plays in Johnson's allegory, but Johnson may well have taken the germ of his idea from Cebes' *Table*.

[25] Edwin C. Heinle, by presenting diagrams of the two allegorical mountains in the appendix to his "Eighteenth-Century Allegorical Essay", brings out the similarity more strikingly than one can with a verbal comparison. Heinle goes so far as to state that 'the model' for the roads running up Johnson's 'Mountain of Existence' is undoubtedly the long road of Cebes (p. 141).

[26] John Healey, trans., Epictetus' *Manuall;* Cebes' *Table;* Theophrastus' *Characters* (London, 1616), p. 139.

VI

THE *RAMBLER* ALLEGORIES

"An allegorical history of Rest and Labour" is the title that was given in 1752, presumably by Johnson himself, to *Rambler* No. 33. The term 'allegorical history' might have been with equal justice also applied to the allegory of Criticism in *Rambler* No. 3, as well as to the allegories in *Rambler* Nos. 22, 91, and 96. The characteristic which sets these allegories apart from most others is that the organizing principle is time rather than space.

The first of Johnson's allegories in the *Rambler* (No. 3) occurs in the second part of an essay which begins by describing the difficulty of the task of an author and the malevolence and presumption of critics. The allegory which follows is in more than one way an illustration of what precedes it. Once again, Johnson gives us his meaning before his fable, by stating in the sentence directly before its introduction that many who call themselves critics "have presumed upon a forged commission, styled themselves the ministers of criticism, without any authentick evidence of delegation, and uttered their own determinations, as the decrees of a higher judicature".[1] Moreover, the allegory itself is a perfect example of that part of the task of an author which we are told in the first portion of the essay is

to vary the dress and situation of common objects, so as to give them fresh grace and more powerful attractions; to spread such flowers over the regions through which the intellect has already made its progress, as may tempt it to return, and take a second view of things hastily passed over, or negligently regarded.[2]

The organization of the allegory according to time rather than space gives Johnson the opportunity to present a contrast between

[1] *Works*, II, 12.
[2] *Works*, II, 11.

things as they ought to be and things as they are in terms of a contrast between the past and the present. But Johnson is not proposing reforms; he is interested solely in showing each thing in its true light. He is not distressed that the world is not perfect, but he does know the meaning of perfection.

The allegory first describes the perfect function of criticism by referring to a time when the goddess Criticism walked the earth, viewing works with 'the torch of truth' and passing sentence upon them with 'the sceptre of justice'. The present state of criticism can be explained only if we conceive that the goddess Criticism has withdrawn her presence from the earth and that flattery and malevolence have taken her place. But we must not imagine that they also have her power, for it is easily seen that "time passes his sentence at leisure, without any regard to their determinations".[3]

There is no indication that the present state is to be lamented. On the contrary, the proceedings of time are "conformable to justice", and Criticism is still able "to shed her influence from afar upon some select minds, fitted for its reception by learning and by virtue".[4] Nevertheless it is still necessary to understand the true nature of criticism in order not to be deceived by the imposture of those who take her name.

Johnson's allegory conveys all this with a minimum of apparatus. Its imagery consists of almost nothing but a sceptre and a torch. The sceptre, to be sure, is as elaborate as any we find in the most picturesque allegories, a sceptre, "one end of which was tinctured with ambrosia, and inwreathed with a golden foliage of amaranths and bays: the other end was encircled with cypress and poppies, and dipped in the waters of oblivion".[5] But sceptres may be ornate without being ridiculous. The description of abstract beings is an entirely different matter.

The personifications in *Rambler* No. 3 would surely be classified as 'non-restrictive' by Professor Bronson, and the most important of them aside from Criticism herself, the figure of Time, is personified to no greater degree than it often is in common speech. The description of Criticism consists chiefly of an allegorical genealogy of the sort that O. F. Christie must surely have had in mind when he wrote of Johnson's allegories, "Tedious indeed are the personi-

[3] *Works*, II, 15.
[4] *Works*, II, 14.
[5] *Works*, II, 12—13.

fications, and tedious their pedigrees, connections, and employ-ments."[6] I do not know how to answer Christie other than by saying I do not find them so. On the contrary, the pedigrees enable Johnson to convey with great economy the relationships among the con-cepts he discusses. We learn a good deal about the nature of cri-ticism when we hear that Criticism "was the eldest daughter of labour and of truth", that "she was at her birth committed to the care of justice, and brought up by her in the palace of wisdom", and that "she was appointed the governess of fancy".[7] Johnson is interested in delineating the origin and function of criticism, not in presenting an isolated picturesque figure.

In *Rambler* No. 22 ("An allegory on wit and learning") the con-trast which is represented in terms of different time-periods is that between wit and learning in concord and wit and learning in strife. It is a contrast that is for the most part implicit, for through-out the body of the allegory we see Wit and Learning continually engaged in battle. Only in the last paragraph of the allegory do we learn that Wit and Learning "lived afterwards in perpetual concord" and eventually "married at the command of Jupiter, and had a numerous progeny of arts and sciences".[8]

The sequence of a period of discord followed by a period of con-cord is the reverse of what we would normally expect in an alle-gory structured upon time. In both *Rambler* No. 3 and No. 33 Johnson establishes his contrast by BEGINNING with a description of a period of harmony that we may take as a golden age from which the world has since fallen. In *Rambler* No. 22 we may wonder for a moment whether Johnson does not have things backwards. Ostensibly, his allegory tells us that the opposition between wit and learning ceased centuries ago. But if we look at the allegory closely, it is clear that the discord between wit and learning has been resolved only in heaven, not on earth. It was during the period when Wit and Learning were still at strife that they visited the earth "and carried on their ancient quarrel among mortals".[9] And we must assume that it is still being carried on among mortals.

[6] O. F. Christie, *Johnson The Essayist* (New York, George H. Doran Co., 1925), p. 123.
[7] *Works*, II, 12.
[8] *Works*, II, 113.
[9] *Works*, II, 112.

The point of the allegory is that an ancient quarrel which was long ago resolved still continues among men.

There is, though, another possible interpretation of the sequence of events in Johnson's allegorical history. It may be that Johnson meant to indicate that the famous quarrels between wit and learning – between poets such as Pope and scholars such as Theobald – of the generation before his own had at last been resolved in his maturer age, and could be looked back upon as something ridiculous.

At any rate, it is a quarrel among men, not gods, and not abstractions that Johnson is talking about. As a result, *Rambler* No. 22 of all Johnson's allegories comes nearest to the technique of the Theophrastan Character. Consider the following description of the actions of Wit and Learning:

Wit was daring and adventurous; learning cautious and deliberate. Wit thought nothing reproachful but dullness; learning was afraid of no imputation but that of errour. Wit answered before he understood, lest his quickness of apprehension should be questioned; learning paused, where there was no difficulty, lest any insidious sophism should lie undiscovered. Wit perplexed every debate by rapidity and confusion; learning tired the hearers with endless distinctions, and prolonged the dispute without advantage, by proving that which never was denied. Wit, in hopes of shining, would venture to produce what he had not considered, and often succeeded beyond his own expectation, by following the train of a lucky thought; learning would reject every new notion, for fear of being entangled in consequences which she could not foresee, and was often hindered, by her caution from pressing her advantages, and subduing her opponent.[10]

If in such a group of sentences we were to substitute 'the wit' and 'the learned man' for 'wit' and 'learning' and convert the whole to the present tense, the result would be a double, but otherwise regular, and masterfully executed, Theophrastan Character.

Of all Johnson's allegorical histories, *Rambler* No. 33 ("An allegorical history of Rest and Labour") comes closest to beginning with a conventional description of a golden age. The allegory describes a time "in the early ages of the world" when "mankind was happy in the enjoyment of continual pleasure, and constant plenty, under the protection of rest".[11] While such a subject remains in focus, Johnson's allegory is as rich in imagery as the most picturesque canto in Spenser. Johnson luxuriates in depicting 'shades of

[10] *Works*, II, 110—111.
[11] *Works*, II, 161.

jasmine and myrtle', 'rivers flowing with milk and nectar', 'the fragrance of perpetual spring', 'bowers arched by nature', 'birds singing', 'beasts sporting', and so forth, for the pure pleasure that such images can give.[12]

But Johnson's allegorical histories depend upon contrast. The allegory makes it clear that such a paradise did not long remain free from corruption. Johnson goes on to describe how "the state of the earth was changed" in such a way that "the year was divided into seasons" and "part of the ground became barren".[13] In such a world men soon found that Rest is "an impotent and deceitful goddess", who resigns her worshippers to "the first attacks of either famine or disease, and suffers her shades to be invaded by every enemy, and destroyed by every accident".[14] And so men responded to the call of Labour.

That gives Johnson yet another stage of the world to describe. With the help of Labour

the face of things was immediately transformed; the land was covered with towns and villages, encompassed with fields of corn, and plantations of fruit-trees; and nothing was seen but heaps of grain, and baskets of fruit, full tables, and crowded storehouses.[15]

Johnson indeed engages the figure of Labour in 'real employment'. Nevertheless, Johnson is still careful to avoid 'ascribing effects to non-entity'. When Labour turns up the earth, he does it with 'the implements of husbandry'; when he raises walls and towers, he uses 'the tools of architecture'.[16] It is with 'the instruments of labour' that the landscape is transformed.

But Johnson is not done, for he would have men give themselves neither wholly to labor nor wholly to rest. Labour, it was found, could not prevent the approach of Lassitude; nor could Rest enjoy the fruits of Labour for very long before the approach of Satiety. Labour and Rest, therefore, at last "agreed to divide the world between them, and govern it alternately, allotting the dominion of the day to one, and that of the night to the other, and promised to guard the frontiers of each other, so that, whenever hostilities were attempted, satiety should be intercepted by labour, and lassi-

---

[12] *Works*, II, 161.
[13] *Works*, II, 161.
[14] *Works*, II, 162.
[15] *Works*, II, 163.
[16] *Works*, II, 162.

tude expelled by rest".[17] What is more, "rest afterwards became pregnant by labour, and was delivered of health, a benevolent goddess, who consolidated the union of her parents, and contributed to the regular vicissitudes of their reign, by dispensing her gifts to those only who shared their lives in just proportions between rest and labour".[18] As in *Rambler* No. 3, Johnson ends with the world as it is, and he is content to leave it as it is however it may differ from the idealized world with which he began.

Differing in structure from the first three *Rambler* allegories, *Rambler* No. 65 ("Obidah and the hermit; an eastern story") is a combination of allegory and oriental tale. Or is combination the wrong word? For the two are hardly combined, although they are joined in a single essay. The essay presents an oriental tale with an allegory tacked on to its end. The allegory, to be sure, is nothing more than an interpretation of the tale, but the tale is not necessarily allegorical without the interpretation. While the tale of Obidah's day's journey clearly enough points a moral, its images of bowers and shades and gardens do not strike us as metaphors until, when the tale itself is over, we hear a hermit interpret them as 'bowers of ease', 'shades of security', and 'gardens of pleasure' as he explains that "human life is the journey of a day".[19]

The allegory is not one of Johnson's best. Except for the bilingual pun on the word 'errours', which has already been pointed out, and a more obvious pun on 'the *ways* of virtue', its metaphors are not very striking. But if it is correct to look upon *Rasselas* as a combination of oriental tale and allegory, *Rambler* No. 65 must be numbered among its definite precursors.

With the allegory of the Garden of Hope in *Rambler* No. 67, Johnson returns to the more familiar allegorical style of "The Vision of Theodore". His allegory is once again cast as a dream-vision, and his dreamer is again subject to the same human weakness as those he observes: in this case, the weakness of deceiving oneself with the false promises of hope. The dreamer relates, "though I pressed onward with great celerity, I was still in sight of pleasures of which I could not yet gain the possession, and which seemed to mock my

---

[17] *Works*, II, 165.
[18] *Works*, II, 165.
[19] *Works*, II, 312.

diligence, and to retire as I advanced".[20] There is even in the allegory of the Garden of Hope, like Mt. Teneriffe in "The Vision of Theodore", "an eminence" which affords "a more extensive view of the whole place", although this time, significantly, it is within the place and not apart from it.[21] Indeed every figure of the allegory exists within the larger metaphor of the Garden of Hope, just as in "The Vision of Theodore" all of the figures except Mt. Teneriffe have their place within the similarly encompassing metaphor of the Mountain of Existence.

But there is a certain characteristic which sets the allegory in *Rambler* No. 67 apart from "The Vision of Theodore" and the other allegories we have examined so far. I call attention to it because it may help us to understand Johnson's technique later in *Rasselas*. Within the obviously allegorical Garden of Hope, we meet several characters who do not seem to be allegorical at all. The man who "had been twenty years soliciting" a place which "would soon be vacant", the man "who was departing in haste to take possession of the estate of an uncle, who by the course of nature could not live long", another who "was preparing to dive for treasure in a new-invented bell", and the man who "was on the point of discovering the longitude"[22] are all, to be sure, representative examples of men made ridiculous by false hope and therefore are fitting inhabitants of the Garden of Hope. But such characters are clearly not allegorical embodiments of hope in the way that the youthful goddess whom we later see sitting on a throne in the Garden is. They are much more like the inhabitants of the Happy Valley or the characters that Rasselas and his party meet on their journey. And however circular the reasoning process may seem, the fact that Johnson introduces such non-allegorical characters into an allegorical framework in *Rambler* No. 67 gives us reason to suspect that the framework of *Rasselas* may be allegorical although its characters are not.

Another *Rambler* allegory which, like *Rambler* No. 67, places allegorical and non-allegorical figures alongside one another within a dream framework might also be mentioned here. In *Rambler* No. 105 ("The universal register: a dream"), the figures of Justice, Truth, and Curiosity are allegorical embodiments of the qualities their names signify, but the men who approach the office of the

[20] *Works*, II, 318—319.
[21] *Works*, II, 320.
[22] *Works*, II, 319.

universal register are to be taken only as representative men made ridiculous, this time not by false hopes but by unjust pretensions.

If it was Johnson himself – and there is no reason to assume otherwise – who later supplied the titles for the *Rambler* essays, it may be significant that *Rambler* Nos. 105 and 67 are both subtitled 'a dream' rather than 'an allegory'. Johnson seems to have reserved the latter term for only those pieces which would be considered allegories according to the strictest definition.

An aspect of Johnsonian allegory which is discernible to some degree in many of the pieces examined so far is most fully pronounced in the allegory of Patronage which comprises *Rambler* No. 91. I would call that aspect 'the mock-allegoric'. I mean by the term a manner of allegory completely analogous to the mock-heroic manner in epic or novel, which, as we know, attained its greatest popularity in the eighteenth century.

Johnson often reminds us that the function of a comparison is either to illustrate or aggrandize, that a simile to be perfect should not only clarify, but also ennoble a subject, "display it to the fancy with greater dignity".[23] If Johnson does not stress that allegory must do the same, the reason is only that he felt allegory could not possibly do otherwise. The form of allegory like that of the epic had for so many centuries been employed upon exalted subject matter that its mere use had become a claim to dignity.

But Johnson also points out that what is little "by claiming dignity becomes ridiculous".[24] Pope and Fielding had discovered that by employing the epic machinery of heroic poetry to describe trivial events they could make them seem ridiculous and ludicrous. As Professor Maynard Mack points out, the mock-heroic structure performs the double function of emphasizing the 'epic proportions' to which society magnifies its trifles and of revealing their real triviality.[25] The intention, it should be clearly understood, is not to mock the devices of epic poetry but to expose affectation. Johnson, without ever mocking allegorical conventions, often uses allegory for a similar purpose. For example, a large part of the humor of *Rambler* No. 22 comes from the realization that what is

[23] "Life of Pope", *Lives*, III, 229. Cf. definition of 'simile' in *Dictionary*.
[24] "Life of Cowley", *Lives*, I, 45.
[25] Maynard Mack, Introduction to *The Augustans*, 2nd ed. (Englewood Cliffs, N. J., Prentice-Hall, Inc., 1961), p. 25.

described as a serious battle between allegorical beings is nothing more than a senseless quarrel between pedants and so-called wits. Similarly, in *Rambler* No. 3 the description of the present state of literary criticism in terms of universal history has a somewhat ludicrous effect, which should not be missed.

Johnson's mock-allegoric manner is most readily apparent in his allegory of Patronage. Patronage, it is true, is "but half a goddess",[26] but that is enough of a claim to dignity to make her appear ridiculous. For Johnson's Patronage is nothing more than a patron, and in fact bears a striking resemblance to the character of Aurantius the literary patron in *Rambler* No. 163.

The mock-allegoric effect is sustained by numerous devices. As the patron is made a goddess, his residence is as easily converted to a palace. The patron's familiar – too familiar – antechamber is designated "the *hall of expectation*".[27] The patron's capriciousness becomes the goddess Caprice, who controls the inner doors by which one gains access to Patronage. By dozens of such touches, Johnson makes use of the incongruous contrast between the allegorical manner and real life to expose the pompousness and pettiness of patrons. The effect is humorous, but behind the humor we cannot help hearing the voice of sad experience:

Seven years, My Lord, have now past since I waited in your outward Rooms or was repulsed from your Door, during which time I have been pushing on my work through difficulties of which It is useless to complain, and have brought it at last to the verge of Publication without one Act of assistance, one word of encouragement, or one smile of favour. Such treatment I did not expect, for I never had a Patron before.[28]

Johnson's allegory of Truth, Falsehood, and Fiction in *Rambler* No. 96 shares certain characteristics with a number of the allegories already examined. As in *Rambler* No. 3, the allegory, which occurs in the latter portion of the essay, is an illustration of what Johnson has said first in non-allegorical prose. In the first part of the essay, we are told that men hear truth unwillingly because it is generally "contrary to our wishes, and opposite to our practice",

[26] *Works*, II, 427.
[27] *Works*, II, 428.
[28] Letter to the Earl of Chesterfield (February 7, 1755), *The Letters of Samuel Johnson*, ed. R. W. Chapman (Oxford, Clarendon Press, 1952), I, 64.

and that to overcome the reluctance against truth "precepts have been hidden under a thousand appearances".[29] In the allegory, we are shown a figure of Truth who "obstructed her own progress by the severity of her aspect, and the solemnity of her dictates", and who, that "she might obtain an easier reception", was invested by the Muses with "a loose and changeable robe, like that in which falsehood captivated her admirers" and under such guise, was named Fiction.[30] We understand from the allegory that "the legitimate end of fiction is the conveyance of truth".[31]

The structure of the allegory itself most closely resembles that of *Rambler* No. 22. As in each of the first three *Rambler* allegories, the organization is according to time rather than space, but, as in *Rambler* No. 22, the initial age described is one of discord instead of harmony. The battles between Falsehood and Truth, which occupy a large portion of the allegory, are reminiscent of the skirmishes between Wit and Learning.

If we wish to search for allegorical puns in *Rambler* No. 96, we might pause over the clause, "and the quiver of sophistry rattled on her shoulder", describing Falsehood as she engages in battle with Truth.[32] A quiver, of course, as Johnson's *Dictionary* tells us, is 'a case or sheath for arrows'. But there is a verb *to quiver* as well, for which Johnson gives the definition 'to quake; to play with a tremulous motion'. Possibly there is an intended pun in Johnson's phrase 'the quiver of sophistry': might not 'quiver' refer to the 'quaking' of sophistry as well as to the case of arrows which the figure of Falsehood carries on her shoulder? If it does, we have at last found in Johnson's allegories an example of a pun upon a pair of genuine homonyms rather than merely different meanings of the same word.

Of the *Rambler* allegories, the allegory of the Ocean of Life, which already has served to provide us with some good examples of allegorical puns, is the most comprehensive, the most profound, and the most Johnsonian in theme.

I suppose we may say that the basic theme in Johnson's work is that the human condition is everywhere the same. But a basic

[29] *Works*, II, 454.
[30] *Works*, II, 457.
[31] "Life of Waller", *Lives*, I, 271.
[32] *Works*, II, 455.

theme is by definition a theme on which one builds. If the human condition is everywhere the same, why does every man persist in believing in the uniqueness of his own situation? Whatever the reason, that is the peculiarity which makes man interesting to Johnson – interesting enough to write about. It is the problem which occupies much of Johnson's attention in *Rasselas* and almost all of it within the smaller scope of *Rambler* No. 102.

In a way the Ocean of Life is the opposite of the Happy Valley. In the Happy Valley Rasselas believes everyone to be happy but himself; in the Ocean of Life everyman thinks himself to be safe even as he sees others sinking. But in either situation the same characteristic of humanity is brought to light: men are either unable or unwilling to see the similarities between the experiences of others and their own.

The paragraph in *Rambler* No. 102 which expresses the theme most clearly is the following:

It was, however, not very common to steer with much care or prudence; for by some universal infatuation, every man appeared to think himself safe, though he saw his consorts every moment sinking round him; and no sooner had the waves closed over them, than their fate and their misconduct were forgotten; the voyage was pursued with the same jocund confidence; every man congratulated himself upon the soundness of his vessel, and believed himself able to stem the whirlpool in which his friend was swallowed, or glide over the rocks on which he was dashed: nor was it often observed that the sight of a wreck made any man change his course; if he turned aside for a moment, he soon forgot the rudder, and left himself again to the disposal of chance.[33]

Johnson does not attempt to explain the source of this 'universal infatuation', but he is certain of the conclusion to be drawn from it. The allegory ends with an admonition reminiscent of several we have heard before:

"Gaze not idly upon others, when thou thyself art sinking. Whence is this thoughtless tranquillity, when thou and they are equally endangered?"[34]

---

[33] *Works*, II, 483.
[34] *Works*, II, 486.

VII

"BORDERLINE CASES"

Professor Angus Fletcher in his recent broadly comprehensive study of allegory points out that, on the one hand, "we must be ready to discern in almost any work at least a small degree of allegory" and that, on the other hand, "no 'pure allegory' will ever be found".[1] In short, he strongly suggests that in any presentation of examples of the allegorical mode 'borderline cases' may indeed be the norm.[2] It seems therefore that it would not be out of place in the present study if attention be directed to a few of Johnson's works which according to our own working definition of allegory could be considered only 'borderline cases'. Or it might even be profitable to examine one or two works by Johnson which do not, according to our understanding of the term, qualify at all as allegories, but which on occasion have been referred to as allegorical by one or another commentator.

Let us begin with Johnson's fable of the vultures in *Idler* No. 22,[3] which receives the attention of Ellen Douglass Leyburn in her book *Satiric Allegory*. Professor Leyburn is careful to admit that "at first the essay seems not allegorical at all since the animals are not acting in a way that parallels man's actions",[4] but she feels nevertheless that it warrants consideration as an example of an

---

[1] Angus Fletcher, *Allegory: The Theory of a Symbolic Mode* (Ithaca N. Y., Cornell University Press, 1964), p. 8.

[2] Fletcher, p. 10.

[3] This is the original *Idler* No. 22, which was not included in the collected edition. According to the editors of the Yale edition of the *Idler and Adventurer*, Johnson suppressed the essay "probably because of its misanthropic tone". (p. 317, n. 1.) The essay was reprinted by six different newspapers and magazines within the first two months after its initial appearance.

[4] Ellen Douglass Leyburn, *Satiric Allegory: Mirror of Man* (New Haven, Yale University Press, 1956), p. 59.

allegorical satire.[5] The fable, we may recall, introduces us to an old vulture who is instructing her young in the arts of a vulture's life. She explains,

Two herds of men will often meet and shake the earth with noise, and fill the air with fire. When you hear noise and see fire which flashes along the ground, hasten to the place with your swiftest wing, for men are surely destroying one another; you will then find the ground soaking with blood and covered with carcasses, of which many are dismembered and mangled for the convenience of the vulture.[6]

When her pupil interrupts to ask why, when men have killed their prey, they do not eat it, the old vulture answers,

Man . . . is the only beast who kills that which he does not devour, and this quality makes him so much a benefactor to our species.[7]

Still not satisfied, the young vulture remarks, "I would gladly know the reason of this mutual slaughter. I could never kill what I could not eat." But the old vulture can only reply, "My child, . . .this is a question which I cannot answer, tho' I am reckoned the most subtile bird of the mountain."[8]

The fable, perhaps, would be more properly classified as a version of pastoral than as an allegory. The vultures, like the shepherds in a pastoral, provide a removed standpoint from which to comment upon the actions of men of the world. The vultures' lack of knowledge, like the naiveté of shepherds, serves to emphasize the incomprehensibility of men's actions. But the use of animals instead of shepherds as commentators has the advantage of making it especially clear that the satire is directed against mankind in general rather than merely city life or courtly manners.

The fable presents no allegorical beings, no personified abstractions. Yet Professor Leyburn considers the piece an allegory because she feels, "it turns out that the point of view itself is an allegory of man's assumption that he is the center of the universe, with all other beings created for his benefit". She adds, "This attitude of the vultures, which is perfectly sustained . . . contri-

---

[5] As far as I am able to determine, Professor Leyburn uses the terms 'allegorical satire' and 'satiric allegory' interchangeably.

[6] *Idler and Adventurer*, p. 319.

[7] *Idler and Adventurer*, p. 319.

[8] *Idler and Adventurer*, p. 319.

butes an extra level to the irony of the analysis of the reasons why men kill each other for the 'convenience of the vulture'."[9]

I think Professor Leyburn's view is essentially correct, but she might have indicated that the analogy which Johnson draws between his vultures and men extends even further. For a large part of Johnson's fable is a continued metaphor depicting man as a beast of prey. The vulture speaks of man in a vocabulary consisting of such words as '*herds* of men', 'carcasses', 'killed their *prey*', 'the only *beast* who kills that which he does not *devour*', 'remain for a long time quiet in his *den*', 'slaughter', and so forth.

The definitions of these words in Johnson's *Dictionary* make it clear that they are ordinarily used in a sense pertaining exclusively to animals. But for many of these words Johnson is able to record common metaphorical uses as well. The word *herd*, according to the *Dictionary*, designates not only 'A number of beasts together' but also 'A company of men, in contempt or detestation'. Johnson defines *carcass* as 'A dead body of any animal' but recognizes that it is sometimes used 'in a ludicrous sense' to refer to the human body. The two senses of *prey* are made clear by one of the supporting illustrations which Johnson includes with his definition of the word:

> There are men of *prey*, as well as beasts and birds of *prey*, that live upon, and delight in blood. (L'Estrange)[10]

Devour carries the specific meaning, 'To eat up ravenously, as a wild beast or animal of prey' and also the more general sense, 'To enjoy with avidity'. And for beast, Johnson gives the definition, 'A brutal savage man; a man acting in any manner unworthy of a reasonable creature' as well as the literal meaning, 'An animal, distinguished from birds, insects, fishes, and man'.

Johnson, in characteristic style, makes use of his fable of the vultures to give the literal and metaphorical meanings of these words in a single context. The use of terms that we normally associate with animals seems entirely appropriate when we consider that the narrator is a vulture. But the effect of the application of those terms to human beings is to make us see man as a vicious kind of beast. *Idler* No. 22 is much more than 'an allegory of man's

---

[9] Leyburn, p. 59.
[10] *Dictionary*.

assumption that he is the center of the universe'; it is a bitter allegory of man's bestiality.

Mr. Edwin C. Heinle, who does not include *Idler* No. 22, or for that matter *Rambler* Nos. 3, 22, and 96, on the supposedly complete list of allegorical essays of the eighteenth century which he has compiled, does recognize as allegories both Johnson's oriental tale in *Idler* No. 99 and Johnson's fairy tale *The Fountains*.[11]

The tale of Ortogrul of Basra, which comprises *Idler* No. 99, is classified as an allegory by Mr. Heinle apparently because of the account it includes of Ortogrul's dream, which takes up approximately one-third of the tale's length. Ortogrul dreams that he is "ranging a desert country in search of some one that might teach him to grow rich". As Ortogrul stands on the top of a hill, his father appears and directs his view first to 'a torrent tumbling down the rocks, roaring with the noise of thunder, and scattering its foam on the impending woods' and then to 'a little well, out of which issued a small rivulet'. Ortogrul's father then asks him, "dost thou wish for sudden affluence, that may pour upon thee like the mountain torrent, or for a slow and gradual encrease, resembling the rill gliding from the well?" Ortogrul first replies, "Let me be quickly rich, . . .let the golden stream be quick and violent." But then

Ortogrul looked, and perceived the channel of the torrent dry and dusty; but following the rivulet from the well, he traced it to a wide lake, which the supply, slow and constant, kept always full.

And the reader is told that Ortogrul "waked, and determined to grow rich by silent profit, and persevering industry".[12]

---

[11] Edwin C. Heinle, "The Eighteenth-Century Allegorical Essay" (dissertation, Columbia University, 1957), p. 213. *Rambler* Nos. 3 and 96 are omitted from Heinle's list apparently because the essays are not allegorical in their entiretiy: in each the allegory occurs only in the latter half as an illustration of what has gone before. But I can discern no reason at all for Heinle's omission of the allegory of Wit and Learning which comprises the entirety of *Rambler* No. 22. I might also here caution the reader that Harry Alan Ebeling in his "Allegorical Tales of Samuel Johnson" (dissertation, University of Kansas, 1965) discusses as an example of Johnson's allegory *Rambler* No. 44, which he is apparently unaware was written by Mrs. Elizabeth Carter.

[12] *Idler and Adventurer*, p. 304.

The account is surely allegorical in part. Yet the father's question, "dost thou wish for sudden affluence, that may pour upon thee like the mountain torrent, etc." seems to convert the dream's basic metaphor to a simile, causing the effect of allegory to be lost. The mountain torrent and the small rivulet, for the moment, cease to be allegorical and become merely illustrations. But this is so only if we fail to recognize that the word *affluence* in this context is one of Johnson's cleverest allegorical puns. The word is defined in Johnson's *Dictionary* in the following manner:

1. The act of flowing to any place; concourse. It is almost always used figuratively.
2. Exuberance of riches; stream of wealth; plenty.

The first entry reminds us that the word *affluence* has a literal sense which is fully appropriate to Johnson's tale of the torrent and the rivulet, and also tells us that the word was almost never used in its literal sense. Johnson's fable, then, restores literal meaning to what clearly had become a dead metaphor by Johnson's time. The result, as usual, is the creation of an allegorical pun: the word *affluence* is heard as tenor and vehicle at once.

The last of Johnson's works included by Heinle in his list of allegorical essays of the eighteenth century is the fairy tale *The Fountains*, which Johnson contributed in 1766 to Anna Williams' *Miscellanies in Prose and Verse*. On first reading, *The Fountains* seems to be more purely allegorical than the other 'borderline cases' we have been examining in the present chapter. The fountains of the title are quite clearly allegorical metaphors: "the one is called the spring of joy, the other of sorrow".[13] And we find, appropriately, that the waters of joy are sweet and the waters of sorrow bitter. We begin to wonder whether *The Fountains* is properly called an allegory only when we attempt to uncover the allegorical meaning of the whole tale.

The fairy tale belongs to the familiar variety of fable in which a mortal is granted a certain number of wishes, which may be used for good or ill. But Johnson alters the usual pattern of such tales by making the wishes reversible. The fairy Lilinet, as she offers Floretta her gift, explains,

The former gifts of fairies, though bounties in design, have proved commonly mischiefs in the event. We have granted mortals to wish according

13 *Works*, IX, 181.

to their own discretion, and their discretion being small, and their wishes irreversible, they have rashly petitioned for their own destruction. But you, my dearest Floretta, shall have, what none have ever before obtained from us, the power of indulging your wish, and the liberty of retracting it.[14]

Floretta wishes in turn for beauty, 'spirit', wealth, and wit, and Floretta regrets in turn each of those gifts until they are, with the exception of wit, revoked. In the last case, Floretta "resolved to keep her wit, with all its consequences" even though it did not bring happiness.[15] The allegorical meaning here, we might assume, is that wit, unlike beauty, spirit, and wealth, never can be lost. But one does not lose beauty, any more than wit, by wishing it away. The further we try to extend the allegorical meaning of the tale, the less it seems to hold. Surely it cannot be Johnson's message that we may acquire beauty, spirit, wealth, and wit merely by wishing for them. We must either admit that Johnson's allegory here 'breaks' or conclude sensibly that Johnson called *The Fountains* 'a fairy tale' because it was not an allegory.

Johnson employs the fairy-tale device of the wishes to survey various conditions of life, without asking the reader to interpret it as anything more than a device. We must search for the moral of a tale, not the tenor of an allegory, if we wish to arrive at an intelligible interpretation of *The Fountains*. The moral of the tale is easy enough to discover and may be expressed in a single sentence: those gifts which human beings most often wish for do not necessarily bring happiness, and, insofar as they are often the cause of envy, may even entail sorrow.

Aside from Johnson's fables and tales, a large group of Johnson's writings which are sometimes classified as allegories are his Theophrastan Characters. *Rambler* No. 27, for example, which introduces the reader to several type-characters representative of different kinds of literary patrons, is called by Professor Edward Bloom, "one of his [Johnson's] typical allegories".[16] Professor Bloom considers each of the characters a representation of "one of the many vagaries of patronage".[17] His approach to the numerous other brief Characters in Johnson's periodical essays is similar. Bloom is

[14] *Works*, IX, 180.
[15] *Works*, IX, 189.
[16] Edward A. Bloom, "Symbolic Names in Johnson's Periodical Essays", *Modern Language Quarterly*, XIII (December, 1952), 351.
[17] Bloom, p. 351.

quite correct in asking that we consider the names of Johnson's type-characters "as symbols or metaphors whose properties may be extended beyond the immediate contexts in which they appear, and that we interpret them broadly for their generic function".[18] But his use of the word allegory is inexact.

The forms of allegory and Theophrastan Character are closely related but they need not be confused. The Theophrastan Character is defined by the practice of Theophrastus. According to Benjamin Boyce,

The Character as Theophrastus created it is a picture of an imaginary person who represents the group of men possessed by that feature of character (ἦθος) which dominates him.[19]

That definition may be compared with W. T. H. Jackson's of allegory:

It is a sustained narrative in which all, or almost all, of the characters are personifications of abstract qualities which behave like human beings but are always under the dominant influence of the characteristic they represent.[20]

Although Professor Jackson defines allegory too narrowly by restricting it to personification, his definition is here useful in pointing to the difference between allegory and Theophrastan Character. The Character represents a group of men; the personification represents a characteristic. We must view the Character as an abstracted person rather than a personified abstraction. As Professor Leyburn explains, Theophrastan Characters "stand simply for themselves . . . and for all men like them in the particular quality revealed . . . The representation does not have the specific allegorical quality of standing for something other than itself."[21] She is therefore correct in arguing that "we must reluctantly reject as nonallegorical the whole delightfully satiric array of characters, not only those who fall within Boyce's scope, but even their later progeny such as Ned Softly and Tom Folio and Lady Bustle and Beau Tibbs. They are more than themselves in what they represent, but not other than themselves."[22]

[18] Bloom, p. 334.

[19] Benjamin Boyce, *The Theophrastan Character in England to 1642* (Cambridge, Harvard University Press, 1947), p. 152.

[20] W. T. H. Jackson, *The Literature of the Middle Ages* (New York, Columbia University Press, 1960), p. 354.

[21] Leyburn, p. 53.

[22] Leyburn, p. 53.

Rasselas:
THE HAPPY VALLEY AS ALLEGORICAL METAPHOR

A consideration of Samuel Johnson's allegories must not conclude without an examination of *Rasselas* if for no other reason than to correct the impression that the work is an allegory. It is surely unlikely that Johnson, who believed "allegories drawn to great length will always break"[1] – who indeed believed that allegory could not be sustained even in a poem of little more than one-thousand lines (Dryden's *Absalom and Achitophel*) – intended his two volumes of *Rasselas* to be taken as a single, unbroken allegory. Nor do we find in *Rasselas* the allegorical punning and diction so characteristic of Johnson's short allegories. Yet commentators have always considered the work to be 'allegorical', and in recent critical studies we find *Rasselas* referred to by such designations as 'this peculiar conjunction of allegory and anecdote'[2] and 'both a moral fable and an allegorical voyage'.[3]

But *Rasselas* criticism is far more allegorical than *Rasselas*. For literary analysis often tends to allegorize, and all literature, it has been observed, "is from the point of view of commentary more or less allegorical".[4] Yet it is still necessary to distinguish between what is essentially and ostensibly allegorical and what is not. The large portion of *Rasselas* between Rasselas's escape from the Happy Valley and his return to Abyssinia is allegorical only 'from the point of view of commentary'. The critic may say of Rasselas, "He begins by examining two extreme – and opposing – avenues to happi-

---

[1] *Lives*, I, 436–437.

[2] Mary Lascelles, "Rasselas Reconsidered", *Essays and Studies 1951*, ed. Geoffrey Tillotson (London, John Murray), p. 44.

[3] Alvin Whitley, "The Comedy of Rasselas", *ELH*, XXIII (March, 1956), 49.

[4] Angus Fletcher, *Allegory: The Theory of a Symbolic Mode* (Ithaca, N.Y., Cornell University Press, 1964), p. 8.

ness . . .".[5] But Rasselas is still a youth entering the world, not an allegorical figure at a forked path. The allegorical diction is the critic's, not Samuel Johnson's. Another critic writes, "We know Imlac and Rasselas and their female companions as points of view and the unnamed characters whom they encounter as ways of life."[6] But our knowing does not change the nature of Johnson's work. The characters of Rasselas were created as individuals or types, not metaphors. Like Theophrastan characters, "They are more than themselves in what they represent, but not other than themselves."[7]

The Happy Valley, on the other hand, unlike the characters of Rasselas, does seem to represent something other than itself, something other than a type of valley. While the whole of Rasselas, then, is not to be looked upon as an allegory, it is probably safe to say that – or at least reasonable to ask whether – the Happy Valley in Rasselas has the qualities of an allegorical metaphor. Whether it does can be discovered only by seeking to determine of what abstraction it might possibly be the embodiment. Of what metaphor may it be considered the vehicle?

But first we must examine the vehicle. Perhaps no aspect of the study of Rasselas has received more careful scholarly attention in the past decade than the subject of the Ethiopian background of the tale and the sources of the figure of the Happy Valley. Until quite recently it had been generally accepted, and often reiterated, that the Ethiopian background of Rasselas reflected the information which Johnson had acquired at the beginning of his literary career as a result of his translation of Lobo's Voyage to Abyssinia from the French of Joachim Le Grand. Boswell even had called Johnson's early translation "the remote occasion" of his writing Rasselas.[8] And as late as 1940, Harold D. Jenkins stated that the Happy Valley

---

[5] Gwin J. Kolb, "The Structure of Rasselas", PMLA, LXVI (September, 1951), 708.

[6] Ellen Douglass Leyburn, "Two Allegorical Treatments of Man: 'Rasselas' and 'La Peste' ", Criticism 4 (Summer, 1962), p. 199.

[7] Leyburn, Satiric Allegory: Mirror of Man (New Haven, Yale University Press, 1956), p. 53. It seems to me that Professor Leyburn's insistence, in her recent article that Johnson's Rasselas and Camus' La Peste are 'frankly allegories' is in contradiction with the view of allegory she presented in her earlier book.

[8] Life, I, 89.

itself "was undoubtedly inspired by details from Lobo and his commentator le Grand".[9]

It had of course always been recognized that there are certain significant differences between the description of the royal prison of the Abyssinian princes in Lobo and Johnson's picture of the Happy Valley. The account in Lobo of "the Barren summit of *Ambaguexa*" on which "Princes of the Blood-Royal pass'd their melancholy Life, being guarded by Officers who treated them often with great Rigour and Severity"[10] hardly suggests a fertile valley in which princes and princesses spend their lives in luxury and ease. Yet it had been assumed that Johnson simply altered what he found in Lobo to suit his purposes. About a decade ago, Professor Ellen Douglass Leyburn attempted to show that even the alterations which Johnson made could have been suggested by descriptions of various fertile regions which occur elsewhere in Lobo's account.[11]Professor Leyburn concluded that Johnson could have gained all of the information needed for supplying the Ethiopian background of *Rasselas* from his reading of Lobo's work.

Instead of settling the issue, Professor Leyburn's article met with strong rebuttals and sparked a very profitable new search for sources of the Ethiopian background of *Rasselas*. Professor Gwin Kolb and especially Professor Donald Lockhart have shown quite conclusively that Johnson had access to a variety of historical and fictional accounts of Ethiopia, many of which contained detailed information, often disagreeing with Lobo's, concerning the place of confinement of the royal princes.[12] We are now aware that Johnson was following a firmly established tradition when he gave Rasselas's prison the appearance of an earthly paradise.[13] If from no other

[9] Harold D. Jenkins, "Some Aspects of the Background of Rasselas", *Studies In English In Honor of Raphael Dorman O'Leary and Selden Lincoln Whitcomb* (Lawrence, Kansas, University of Kansas, 1940), p. 9.

[10] Jerome Lobo, *A Voyage to Abyssinia*, translated from the French (London, 1735), p. 204.

[11] Ellen Douglass Leyburn, " 'No Romantik Absurdities or Incredible Fictions': The Relation of Johnson's *Rasselas* to Lobo's Voyage to Abyssinia", *PMLA*, LXXX (December, 1955), 1064.

[12] Gwin J. Kolb, "The 'Paradise' in Abyssinia and The 'Happy Valley' In *Rasselas*", *Modern Philology*, LVI (August, 1958); Donald M. Lockhart, " 'The Fourth Son of the Mighty Emperor': The Ethiopian Background of Johnson's *Rasselas*", *PMLA*, LXXVIII (December, 1963).

[13] The word *appearance* is deliberately chosen; we must remember that Johnson's Happy Valley is NOT the earthly paradise it appears to be.

source, Johnson surely would have been acquainted with the tradition from four lines in Milton's *Paradise Lost:*

> Nor, where Abassin kings their issue guard,
> Mount Amara (though this by some supposed
> True Paradise) under the Ethiop line
> By Nilus' head, enclosed with shining rock, . . .

(IV, 280—283)

But, apparently, Johnson did use other sources, for several of the particular features by which Johnson's Happy Valley is differentiated from Lobo's barren summit have been traced by Professor Lockhart to their origins in various narrative accounts included in his "Classified List of Original European Works Containing Information on Ethiopia Published Before 1759".[14] Lockhart attributes the location of the royal prison in a valley instead of on a mountaintop to Francisco Alvares' *Verdadera* (1540), the idyllic natural features of the retreat to Luis de Urreta's *Historia* (1610), and the custom of the emperor's annual visit, to the fictional *Late Travels of S. Giacomo Baratti* (1620).[15] Even Johnson's mountain "of which the summits overhang the middle part"[16] is, according to Lockhart, a modification of the oddly-shaped mountain in Urreta on top of which the royal prison is situated.[17]

Johnson's Happy Valley, then, is not an original fictional creation and certainly not a simple transmutation of Lobo's barren summit. Nor is it a reflection of the description of the royal prison of Amhara found in any single historical source. Johnson obviously endowed his valley with exactly those features which he considered necessary for his purpose, from whatever source they came. Furthermore, there is one characteristic – indeed the centrally important characteristic – of the Happy Valley in *Rasselas* which it holds in common with no other account of the royal prison, either historical or fictional (with the possible exception of Milton's *Paradise Lost*).[18] Johnson's description is the only one in which the princes' place

---

[14] Lockhart, pp. 527—528.
[15] Lockhart, pp. 520, 521, 523.
[16] *Rasselas*, p. 8.
[17] Lockhart, p. 521.
[18] I have in mind the phrase in Milton's description, "though this by some SUPPOSED True Paradise", but Milton means primarily that Mount Amara is not to be confused with Eden, not that it is not a pleasant place. (Emphasis mine.)

of exile has "the appearance of security and delight"[19] and not the reality. Out of his awareness of the double tradition of the royal retreat of Amhara as, on the one hand, a place of luxury and security and on the other, a prison of rigor and severity, Johnson came to the highly original decision of drawing upon both traditions to depict the place of exile as a valley in which life appeared to be idyllic, but whose inhabitants considered themselves as miserable prisoners.[20] One must have both aspects of the valley clearly in mind before attempting to interpret Johnson's metaphor.

The interpretations of the allegorical meaning of *Rasselas* that have been offered in the past have proved unsatisfactory because they have failed to take into consideration the double nature of the Happy Valley. Nicholas Joost indeed makes precisely the error that Milton in *Paradise Lost* cautions against. The Happy Valley is by Professor Joost "supposed true paradise". He believes *Rasselas* has "approximate meaning as an allegory of our First Parents, their seduction from innocence and the results thereof".[21] For Professor Joost, the Happy Valley is the "valley of innocence", and "*Rasselas* is the story of man's loss of moral innocence, his discovery of the vanity of all things of the natural life, and his desire to regain that innocence."[22] But Professor Joost's interpretation considers only the appearance of the valley and ignores the state of its inhabitants. A valley peopled by men 'weary of themselves, and of each other' who 'allure others to a state which they feel to be wretched' out of 'the natural malignity of hopeless misery'[23] hardly suggests Eden and surely does not represent innocence. Professor Joost's interpretation has not convinced many.

What remains the standard interpretation of the allegorical meaning of the Happy Valley was given by Martha P. Conant in 1908. Her interpretation, it appears, has been tacitly accepted by a number of modern critics, many of whom may be unaware of its original source; it has never been directly challenged. She wrote,

[19] *Rasselas*, p. 10.

[20] I here have in mind Rasselas and all his attendants, not the other princes and princesses, who receive little of Johnson's attention.

[21] Nicholas Joost, "Whispers of Fancy; or, the Meaning of *Rasselas*", *Modern Age*, I (Fall, 1957), 166.

[22] Joost, p. 167.

[23] *Rasselas*, p. 63.

the Happy Valley, if we look for the meaning of Johnson's allegory, signifies the environment, whether inherited or self-made, of the extreme optimist. Rasselas has the optimistic temperament . . .[24]

Her interpretation of the allegorical metaphor is not so much
wrong as it is misleading. If Rasselas has the temperament of an
'extreme optimist', so does every youth as he embarks upon the
world:

The youth has not yet discovered how many evils are continually hovering
about us, and when he is set free from the shackles of discipline, looks
abroad into the world with rapture . . .[25]

The virgin whom the last summer released from her governess, and who
is now going between her mother and her aunt to try the fortune of her wit
and beauty, suspects no fallacy in the gay representation. She believes
herself passing into another world, and imagines London as an Elysian
region . . .[26]

The optimism of Rasselas represents nothing but the 'hope of inexperience';[27] it is not – like the optimism of Candide, with which Miss
Conant equates it[28] – the result of any particular doctrine or indoctri-
nation. On the contrary, the sages who were responsible for the
education of Rasselas and the other princes and princesses in the
Happy Valley

told them of nothing but the miseries of publick life, and described all
beyond the mountains as regions of calamity, where discord was always
raging, and where man preyed upon man.[29]

And even Rasselas's personal mentor, Imlac – far from being a
Pangloss – says to him,

The world, which you figure to yourself smooth and quiet as the lake in the
valley, you will find a sea foaming with tempests, and boiling with whirl-

[24] Martha Pike Conant, *The Oriental Tale In England In The Eighteenth
Century* (New York, Columbia University Press, 1908), p. 145.

[25] *Rambler* No. 196, *Works*, III, 410.

[26] *Idler* No. 80, *Idler and Adventurer*, p. 250.

[27] *Rasselas*, p. 78.

[28] Conant, p. 148. Miss Conant, who devotes eleven pages to a comparison
of *Rasselas* and *Candide*, does not mention the parallel that might be drawn
between Johnson's Happy Valley and Voltaire's El Dorado. Each is a seclu-
ded valley in which all of the inhabitants appear to be happy. And perhaps
in both cases the appearance is deceiving, although Voltaire is not so explicit
as Johnson on this point.

[29] *Rasselas*, p. 12.

pools: you will be sometimes overwhelmed by the waves of violence and sometimes dashed against the rocks of treachery.[30]

To be sure, Rasselas does not believe a word his elders say to him. But he ignores their cautionings not because he is an optimist, but because he is a youth. It is true that Rasselas is 'in the twenty-sixth year of his age' when the tale begins, but he has not yet had any adult experiences. And neither he nor anyone else who has yet to embark upon the world is willing to learn, or is indeed capable of learning, from the experience of others. Rasselas is subject to a 'universal infatuation'.

We have already seen one aspect of its operation in Johnson's allegory of the Ocean of Life, where every man "believed himself able to stem the whirlpool in which his friend was swallowed, or glide over the rocks on which he was dashed", and where it was not often observed "that the sight of a wreck made any man change his course".[31] In the case of Rasselas, his subjection to the universal infatuation is even more understandable. Not having embarked far enough upon the ocean of life to see the whirlpools and rocks for himself, he is unable to believe the stories of wrecks which he hears. In an *Idler* essay which appeared less than a month before the publication of *Rasselas*, Johnson reminds us that "what is common and unheeded when it is only seen, becomes remarkable and peculiar when we happen to feel it".[32] How much more justifiable, then, is the 'unheeding' of Rasselas, who not only has never felt hardship but has never even seen it.

The only optimism which Rasselas exhibits is his belief that happiness is somewhere to be found. It is not optimism as Voltaire defines it:

– "What is optimism?" said Cacambo. – "Alas!" said Candide, "it's the mania of maintaining that all is well when one is wretched."[33]

---

[30] *Rasselas*, p. 64. Imlac, like Johnson, sometimes cannot help speaking in allegorical metaphors.

[31] *Rambler* No. 102, *Works*, II, 483.

[32] *Idler* No. 50 (March 31, 1759), *Idler and Adventurer*, p. 156. Professor James L. Clifford gives April 19, 1759 as the publication date of *Rasselas*. ("Some Remarks on *Candide* and *Rasselas*", in *Bicentenary Essays on Rasselas*, ed. Magdi Wahba, Cairo Studies in English, 1959, p. 8.)

[33] Voltaire, *Candide*, a bilingual edition, trans. and ed. Peter Gay (New York, St. Martin's Press, 1963), p. 169.

Rasselas knows when he is wretched. His optimism does not cause him to be blind to his own condition. But his inexperience prevents him from judging rightly of the conditions of others. In the Happy Valley, Rasselas believes that he alone of all the inhabitants is unhappy. And later, in Cairo, he wonders:

what can be the reason that I am more unhappy than any of our friends. I see them perpetually and unalterably chearful, but feel my own mind restless and uneasy.[34]

The truth is that there is not one of all his attendants in the Happy Valley 'who does not lament the hour'[35] when he first entered it, and that the young men of Cairo are as unhappy as Rasselas himself. But if Rasselas is misled by the appearance of gaiety, the appearance is not merely in his own mind. In the Happy Valley, men appear to be happy because they pretend to be happy, hoping to "allure others to a state which they feel to be wretched".[36] And in Cairo, the princess learns, "it is the care of a very great part of mankind to conceal their indigence from the rest".[37] It is no wonder that Rasselas believes happiness to be possessed by others, when others go to such lengths to convince him of it. The tendency of men to hide their own wretchedness is so general that Rasselas himself is sometimes guilty of it. In Cairo, he reveals to Imlac, "I live in crowds of jollity, not so much to enjoy company as to shun myself, and am only loud and merry to conceal my sadness."[38] And even in the Happy Valley, he, at one point, "endeavoured to make others pleased with the state of which he himself was weary".[39]

What Rasselas must learn through experience is that

every man . . . may, by examining his own mind, guess what passes in the minds of others: when you feel that your own gaiety is counterfeit, it may justly lead you to suspect that of your companions not to be sincere.[40]

The chief lesson of experience is that the human condition is every-

[34] *Rasselas*, p. 78.
[35] *Rasselas*, p. 62.
[36] *Rasselas*, p. 63.
[37] *Rasselas*, p. 107.
[38] *Rasselas*, p. 78.
[39] *Rasselas*, p. 20.
[40] *Rasselas*, p. 78.

where the same. There is no more ironic statement in all of *Rasselas* than Pekuah's remark,

For nothing . . . is more common than to call our own condition, the condition of life.[41]

Nothing is less common:

let any man tell his own story, and nothing . . . has ever befallen him according to the common order of things; something has always discriminated his case; some unusual concurrence of events has appeared which made him more happy or more miserable than other mortals . . .[42]

Rasselas has yet to learn from experience that his condition is not unique. But experience does not teach quickly:

We are long before we are convinced that happiness is never to be found, and each believes it possessed by others, to keep alive the hope of obtaining it for himself.[43]

And sometimes experience does not teach at all:

For the hope of happiness . . . is so strongly impressed, that the longest experience is not able to efface it.[44]

The progress of Rasselas is from the hope of inexperience to hope despite experience. Yet what is illustrated is not 'extreme optimism' but human nature.[45]

It would seem, then, more reasonable to interpret the Happy Valley as a valley of inexperience rather than as the environment of the extreme optimist. But we must first examine the smaller details of the Happy Valley to see whether our interpretation of the basic metaphor will hold or break. We must not expect to find

[41] *Rasselas*, p. 197. Professor Alvin Whitley misses the point when he states that Pekuah's remark points to "a fallacy of which all the speakers are supremely guilty". ("The Comedy of *Rasselas*", *ELH*, XXIII, 67.) The trouble is that they are NOT guilty of it.

[42] *Idler* No. 50 (March 31, 1759), *Idler and Adventurer*, p. 156.

[43] *Rasselas*, p. 78.

[44] *Rasselas*, p. 98.

[45] Cf. *Rambler* No. 67: "There is no temper so generally indulged as hope: other passions operate by starts on particular occasions, or in certain parts of life; but hope begins with the first power of comparing our actual with our possible state, and attends us through every stage and period, always urging us forward to new acquisitions, and holding out some distant blessing to our view, promising us either relief from pain, or increase of happiness." (*Works*, II, 317.)

a metaphorical equivalent for every single physical detail of the Happy Valley, for most of the natural and artificial features of the valley described in the first chapter of *Rasselas* – the mountains with overhanging summits, the cavern concealed by a thick wood, the gates of iron – indicate nothing more than the valley's remoteness from the world of men. On the other hand, if we take a hint from *Rambler* No. 196, which to a certain extent may be considered a paradigm of the whole of *Rasselas* – a much closer paradigm than *Rambler* Nos. 204–205, which are so often mentioned as such – these features of the valley might well be interpreted to represent 'the shackles of discipline'.[46]

But we must beware of supplying for particular details in *Rasselas* metaphorical equivalents which make no sense, or nonsense, when related to the whole. Consider Nicholas Joost's suggestion that

the episode . . . in which Rasselas and his party leave the happy valley for the greater world, by tunneling through the mountainside enclosing the happy valley, is a plain if unintended allegory of the birth experience.[47]

His interpretation of the episode can only confuse our understanding of what precedes and follows it. The Happy Valley does not represent a womb, and Rasselas's escape from the valley clearly signifies the entry of youth into society, not the entry of the human being into life. Nor do I think that during the account of the escape the analogy of the birth experience comes into the head of any reader of *Rasselas* who does not happen to be looking for it. No interpretation of the meaning of the Happy Valley, or of any allegorical metaphor, can be made without a working assumption that its meaning is consistent with its immediate surroundings in the work from which it comes.

It is neither inconsistent nor insignificant that Rasselas is 'in the twenty-sixth year of his age' when we discover him in the Happy Valley. The Happy Valley does not represent the world of childhood. Presumably, Rasselas has spent his childhood in the valley, but for the reader, and for the purpose of allegory, the Happy Valley does not exist until we find Rasselas in it in his twenty-sixth year.[48] Our attention is never drawn to the younger children

[46] *Works*, III, 410.

[47] Joost, p. 166.

[48] Rasselas himself remarks, "In life . . . is not to be counted the ignorance of infancy"; and we must assume that 'infancy' lasts at least twenty

in the valley, and Rasselas's single reference to his own childhood,

inform me how the day may now seem as short as in my childhood, while nature was yet fresh, and every moment shewed me what I never had observed before . . .[49]

describes a state that contrasts sharply with the 'tediousness of time' and 'vacancies of attention' which characterize life in the Happy Valley.[50] Childhood is a time filled with new experiences because it is a time when all experiences are new.[51] But for Rasselas, who is no longer a child and who has not yet entered the world of adults, there is nothing to experience. "Here is neither labour to be endured nor danger to be dreaded."[52] There is indeed nothing to endure and nothing to fear, so that Rasselas's condition has the 'appearance of security and delight'. As a result, men weary with experience look with envy upon such a state and clamor to enter the Happy Valley, that they 'might bid farewell to hope and fear'.[53] But once they gain admittance, they discover that the alternative to enduring the vicissitudes of experience is to 'sit stupid in the gloom of perpetual vacancy'.[54] The Happy Valley is the embodiment of the state of 'tasteless tranquillity'[55] of one who experiences nothing, either because he has not yet entered the world of men or because he has become weary of it.

It is primarily the desire to free himself from such a state, not the optimistic hope of discovering where happiness is to be found,

---

years if 'the true period of human existence' (between the 'ignorance of infancy' and the 'imbecility of age') "may be reasonably estimated at forty years". (*Rasselas*, pp. 22—23.)

[49] *Rasselas*, p. 18.

[50] *Rasselas*, p. 10.

[51] If we happen to wonder why most of the princes and princesses in the Happy Valley do not share Rasselas's depression, we may assume the answer to be that they are younger than Rasselas, who 'was the fourth son of the mighty emperor', and therefore not yet bored with the simple pleasures of nature. As for Rasselas's three older brothers, we can only guess that their nearer prospect of leaving the valley and succeeding to the throne is sufficient to keep them happy. Probably Johnson never gave the matter a thought because his attention was focused on Rasselas.

[52] *Rasselas*, pp. 17—18.

[53] *Rasselas*, p. 61.

[54] *Rasselas*, p. 62.

[55] *Rasselas*, p. 70.

that motivates Rasselas to leave the Happy Valley. When he
first conceives of the prospect of escaping from the valley, he is
simply 'fired with the desire of doing something',[56] no matter what
it may be. The hope of happiness does not move him nearly so
strongly. Similarly, Nekayah begs to join her brother Rasselas
because she is 'equally weary of confinement . . . and not less desi-
rous of knowing what is done or suffered in the world',[57] not because
of any optimistic illusions. And, of course, when the two of them,
with Imlac and Pekuah, do find their way out of the valley, Imlac
himself is 'very joyful at his escape' even though he 'had less
expectation of pleasure in the world'.[58]

"The Importance of Imlac" has been recently called to critical
attention by Agostino Lombardo's stimulating article of that name.
Lombardo feels "it is Imlac rather than Rasselas who is the portrait
of man", and finds in Imlac's willingness to escape from the Happy
Valley with Rasselas and accompany him on his journey "the story
of a hope which remains alive in the teeth of all evidence; a hope of
which Imlac is the first to acknowledge the irrationality, but which,
in spite of everything, draws him into the absurd quest".[59] But it is
more likely that Imlac, in leaving the Happy Valley, is simply following the advice he later gives to Nekayah:

Do not suffer life to stagnate; it will grow muddy for want of motion: com-
mit yourself again to the current of the world.[60]

Life in the Happy Valley, life removed from experience, is stagnant.
The world has many pains, but the Happy Valley has no pleasures.

If that is Johnson's message, one might be troubled, as the critics
have been troubled, by the fact that Rasselas and his party, after
observing the pains of the world, 'return to Abissinia'.[61] But I place
myself on the side of those critics – notably George Sherburn – who
maintain that Rasselas does not return to the Happy Valley, but
only to Abyssinia.[62] To be sure, we might easily conjecture that if

[56] *Rasselas*, p. 20.
[57] *Rasselas*, p. 70.
[58] *Rasselas*, pp. 70–71.
[59] Agostino Lombardo, "The Importance of Imlac", *Bicentenary Essays
on Rasselas*, ed. Magdi Wahba (Cairo Studies in English, 1959), pp. 48–49.
[60] *Rasselas*, p. 157.
[61] *Rasselas*, p. 221.
[62] George Sherburn, "Rasselas Returns – To What ?", *Philological Quarterly*,
XXXVIII (July, 1959), 383–384.

Rasselas and his party return to Abyssinia they will be found by the royal authorities and either be forced to return to imprisonment in the Happy Valley or be killed. But such conjectures are no more relevant to the interpretation of Johnson's allegorical framework than are speculations concerning Rasselas's childhood before the story began. Johnson's tale ends with Rasselas in Cairo waiting for the inundation of the Nile to cease. I believe that if Johnson wished to indicate that Rasselas and his party returned to the Happy Valley he would have told us so. I interpret the title of the last chapter of Rasselas – "The Conclusion In Which Nothing Is Concluded" – to mean that no decision so definite, and presumably final, as returning to the Happy Valley is reached. We are told that "Imlac and the astronomer were contented to be driven along the stream of life without directing their course to any particular port."[63] I presume that Rasselas and his party remain in the world of experience.

The allegory of the Happy Valley teaches us that man craves experience, that his thirst for experience can never be quenched for long. In the Happy Valley, Rasselas asks, "What . . . makes the difference between man and all the rest of the animal creation?" And he finds the answer. He compares himself to the beast of the valley and discovers,

I am hungry and thirsty like him, but when thirst and hunger cease I am not at rest; I am, like him, pained with want, but I am not, like him, satisfied with fulness. The intermediate hours are tedious and gloomy; I long again to be hungry that I may again quicken my attention.[64]

The human being needs "to fill up the vacancies of attention, and lessen the tediousness of time".[65]

The felicity of the Happy Valley, like the felicity of the animals Rasselas observes, "is not the felicity of man".[66] "Man", concludes Rasselas, "has surely some latent sense for which this place affords no gratification, or he has some desires distinct from sense which must be satisfied before he can be happy."[67] The craving which

---

[63] Rasselas, p. 220.
[64] Rasselas, pp. 14—15.
[65] Rasselas, p. 10.
[66] Rasselas, p. 15.
[67] Rasselas, p. 15.

the Happy Valley is incapable of satisfying is not the desire for
sensual experience, but what Johnson terms 'that hunger of the
imagination which preys incessantly upon life, and must be always
appeased by some employment'.[68] Johnson's meaning may be, as
Joseph Wood Krutch suggests, "that man has some desire which
nothing in his experience is capable of satisfying".[69] The diversions
of the world may be able only to appease and not satisfy man's
hunger of the imagination. But Johnson does not therefore recom-
mend that youth should refrain from embarking upon the world
and remain in a state of confinement appropriate only to childhood.
The world cannot satisfy youth's 'hope of uninterrupted happiness', but it offers 'an opportunity of adding knowledge to vivacity,
and enlarging innocence to virtue', which seclusion does not provide.[70] "Ignorance is mere privation, by which nothing can be
produced: it is a vacuity in which the soul sits motionless and torpid
for want of attraction."[71]

Rasselas commits no folly in leaving the Happy Valley. *Rasselas*
is not, as it has been called, 'a satire on the illusioned view of life',[72]
or even 'the story of youthful illusion destroyed by experience'.[73]
The illusions of inexperience are not to be ridiculed and are, fortunately, not easily destroyed. Without them, Johnson once jotted
down, there would be 'no hope – no undertaking – no regard to
benevolence – no fear of disgrace'.[74] Is it not a blessing that youth
does not learn from the experience of age?

...the miseries of life would be increased beyond all human power of
endurance, if we were to enter the world with the same opinions as we
carry from it.[75]

[68] *Rasselas*, p. 145.
[69] Joseph Wood Krutch, *Samuel Johnson* (New York, Henry Holt and
Company, 1944), p. 177.
[70] The phrases are from *Idler* No. 80, which tells of a young virgin's
first trip to London. *(Idler and Adventurer*, pp. 251—252.)
[71] *Rasselas*, p. 56.
[72] Alvin Whitley, p. 51.
[73] Lombardo, p. 48.
[74] *Life*, I, 206.
[75] *Rambler* No. 196, *Works*, III, 410.

A CONCLUDING NOTE

I am tempted to follow the example of Johnson in *Rasselas* and entitle this a 'conclusion in which nothing is concluded'. For I have attempted to prove nothing other than that Samuel Johnson's allegories are skillfully wrought and rewarding to read. Whether I have been successful can be determined only by turning now to Johnson's allegories and reading them with care.

Nevertheless, a study of Johnson's allegories does lead one to draw certain conclusions concerning the mind and art of Johnson, for it inevitably brings one in contact with some of the major questions to which Johnsonian scholars and critics have long been seeking answers. I have in mind specifically the two sister questions of whether Johnson's critical theory calls for generality or particularity in art and whether Johnson's own prose is characterized by abstractness or concrete imagery.

I think that we have already seen that the answer to the first question is that Johnson's critical theory calls for both generality and particularity in art but that Johnson calls for them for different reasons and expects them to be supplied in different ways. We are now prepared to deal with the second, and more complicated, of the two questions: Is Johnson's prose 'non-sensory', 'general', and 'abstract' (Wimsatt's terms) or does it make 'rich use' of 'concrete and vivid imagery' (Greene's terms).

In order to call attention to the particular point of controversy, Professor Donald J. Greene recently, and somewhat whimsically, constructed the following statement: "Metaphors in other writers render the abstract concrete; metaphors in Johnson somehow remain abstract." Professor Greene has formulated the statement as an illustration of what he considers the logical contradiction in the reasoning of Professor Wimsatt and others, who, while granting that Johnson frequently uses figurative language, continue to speak of the abstractness of his prose.[1] According to Greene, such critics fail to see the "vivid concreteness of imagery" in Johnson's metaphors because they refuse to bring to Johnson "the amount of response to imagery which one brings to Shakespeare and Keats'.[2]

But may it not be that Johnson himself controls the amount, or kind, of response to imagery that we bring to his metaphors? I think the supposedly contradictory statement which Greene has formulated, however paradoxical it may be, happens to be correct. From our study of Johnson's allegory we should be able to see exactly how Johnson's metaphors 'remain abstract'. The distinguishing quality of Johnson's metaphors is that they never turn the mind 'more upon that from which the illustration is drawn than that to which it is applied'. For Johnson believed "the force of metaphors is lost, when the mind . . . is turned more upon the original [vehicle] than the secondary [tenor] sense".[3] Concrete is the wrong adjective for Johnson's imagery, for his images never block our view of the abstractions behind them.

The force of allegory is lost when the mind is turned more upon its surface than its substance. Samuel Johnson's allegories are designed for those minds that desire the full force of allegory.

---

[1] Donald J. Greene, " 'Pictures To The Mind': Johnson and Imagery", in *Johnson, Boswell, and Their Circle: Essays Presented to L. F. Powell* (Oxford, Clarendon Press, 1965), p. 158, n. 2.

[2] Greene, pp. 147—148, p. 149.

[3] *Lives*, I, 45.

SELECTED BIBLIOGRAPHY

I. WORKS BY SAMUEL JOHNSON

The Works of Samuel Johnson, LL.D., 11 vols. (Oxford, 1825).

The Yale Edition of the Works of Samuel Johnson. (General editor, Allen T. Hazen) Vol. I: *Diaries, Prayers, and Annals*, edited by E. L. McAdam, Jr., with Donald and Mary Hyde (1958); Vol. II: *The Idler and The Adventurer*, edited by W. J. Bate, J. M. Bullitt, and L. F. Powell (1963); Vol. VI: *Poems*, edited by E. L. McAdam, Jr., with George Milne (1964). (New Haven, Yale University Press.)

A Dictionary of the English Language by Samuel Johnson, LL.D., 2 vols. (6th ed., London, 1785).

The Letters of Samuel Johnson, edited by R. W. Chapman, 3 vols. (Oxford, Clarendon Press, 1952).

Lives of the English Poets by Samuel Johnson, LL.D., edited by George Birkbeck Hill, 3 vols. (Oxford, Clarendon Press, 1905).

Johnson's Notes to Shakespeare, edited by Arthur Sherbo, Augustan Reprint Society Publications Nos. 59—60, 65—66, and 71—73 (Los Angeles, University of California, 1956—1958).

Rasselas, edited by R. W. Chapman (Oxford, Clarendon Press, 1927).

II. OTHER WORKS OF THE EIGHTEENTH CENTURY AND EARLIER

Addison, Joseph, *The Spectator*, edited by George A. Aitken, 6 vols. (London, George Routledge & Sons, Ltd.).

—, *Works*, edited by Richard Hurd, 6 vols (London, 1811).

Aristotle, *Basic Works*, edited by Richard McKeon (New York, Random House, 1941).

—, *On Poetry and Style*, translated by G.M.A. Grube (New York, Liberal Arts Press, 1958).

Boswell, James, *Life of Johnson*, edited by George Birkbeck Hill and revised by L. F. Powell, 6 vols. (Oxford, Clarendon Press, 1934).

—, *The Journal of a Tour to the Hebrides with Samuel Johnson*, edited by L. F. Powell (Revised ed., London, J. M. Dent & Sons, Ltd., 1958).

Burrowes, Robert, "Essay on the Stile of Doctor Johnson", *The Transactions of the Royal Irish Academy* (Dublin, 1787).

Cebes, *Table*, translated by John Healey (London,1616).

Dodsley, Robert, *The Preceptor* (5th ed., London, 1769).

Hughes, John, "On Allegorical Poetry", *in Critical Essays of the Eighteenth Century 1700—1715*, edited by Willard Higley Durham (New Haven, Yale University Press, 1915; New York, Russel & Russell, 1961).

Lobo, Jerome, *A Voyage to Abyssinia*, translated from the French (by Samuel Johnson) (London, 1735).

Pope, Alexander, *Twickenham Edition of the Poems*, Vol. II: *The Rape of the Lock and Other Poems*, edited by Geoffrey Tillotson (3rd ed.; London, Methuen & Co., 1962).

Voltaire, *Candide*, a bilingual edition, translated and edited by Peter Gay (New York, St. Martin's Press, 1963).

III. CRITICAL BOOKS

Bate, Walter Jackson, *The Achievement of Samuel Johnson* (New York, Oxford University Press, 1955).

Boyce, Benjamin, *The Theophrastan Character in England to 1642* (Cambridge, Harvard University Press, 1947).

Chapin, Chester F., *Personification in Eighteenth-Century English Poetry* (New York, Kings' Crown Press, 1955).

Christie, O. F., *Johnson The Essayist* (New York, George H. Doran Co., 1925).

Clifford, James L., *Young Sam Johnson* (New York, McGraw-Hill Book Company, Inc., 1955).

—, *Johnsonian Studies 1887—1950* (Minneapolis, University of Minnesota Press, 1951).

— and Greene, Donald J., *A Bibliography of Johnsonian Studies 1950— 1960*.

Conant, Martha Pike, *The Oriental Tale in England in the Eighteenth Century* (New York, Columbia University Press, 1908).

Empson, William, *Seven Types of Ambiguity* (2nd ed., London, Chatto & Windus, 1947).

Fletcher, Angus, *Allegory: The Theory of a Symbolic Mode* (Ithaca, Cornell University Press, 1964).

Hagstrum, Jean H., *Samuel Johnson's Literary Criticism* (Minneapolis, University of Minnesota Press, 1952).

Heinle, Edwin C., "The Eighteenth-Century Allegorical Essay" (Unpublished Ph. D. dissertation, Columbia University, 1957).

Jackson, W. T. H., *The Literature of the Middle Ages* (New York, Columbia University Press, 1960).

Krutch, Joseph Wood, *Samuel Johnson* (New York, Henry Holt and Company, 1944).

Lewis, C. S., *The Allegory of Love* (London, Oxford University Press, 1936).

Leyburn, Ellen Douglass, *Satiric Allegory: Mirror of Man* (New Haven, Yale University Press, 1956).

Spivack, Bernard, *Shakespeare and the Allegory of Evil* (New York, Columbia University Press, 1958).

Stephen, Leslie, *Samuel Johnson* (London, Macmillan & Co., 1878).

Tate, Allen, *Collected Essays* (Denver, Allan Swallow, 1959).

Tindall, William York, *The Literary Symbol* (New York, Columbia University Press, 1955).

Wimsatt, William K., Jr., *The Prose Style of Samuel Johnson* (New Haven, Yale University Press, 1941).

—, *Philosophic Words: A Study of Style and Meaning in the "Rambler" and "Dictionary" of Samuel Johnson* (New Haven, Yale University Press, 1948).

IV. CRITICAL ARTICLES

Bloom, Edward, A., "The Allegorical Principle". *ELH*, XVIII (September, 1951), 163—190.

—, "Symbolic Names in Johnson's Periodical Essays", *Modern Language Quartely*, XIII (December, 1952), 333—352.

Bronson, Betrand H., "Personification Reconsidered", in *New Light On Dr. Johnson*, edited by Frederick W. Hilles (New Haven, Yale University Press, 1959).

—, Introduction to *Rasselas, Poems and Selected Prose* (New York, Holt, Rinehart and Winston, 1958).

—, "The Double Tradition of Dr. Johnson", in *Eighteenth-Century English Literature: Modern Essays in Criticism*, edited by James L. Clifford (New York, Oxford University Press, 1959).

Clifford, James L., "Some Remarks on *Candide* and *Rasselas*", in *Bicentenary Essays on Rasselas*, edited by Magdi Wahba (Cairo Studies in English, 1959).

Dargan, H. M., "The Nature of Allegory As Used by Swift", *Studies in Philology*, XIII (1916), 159—179.

Emden, Cecil S., "Dr. Johnson and Imagery", *R.E.S.* New Series, I (1950), 23—38.

Fleischauer, Warren L., Introduction to *Rasselas* (Great Neck, N.Y., Barron's Educational Series, Inc., 1962).

Greene, Donald J. " 'Pictures To The Mind': Johnson and Imagery", in *Johnson, Boswell, and Their Circle: Essays Presented to L. F. Powell* (Oxford, Clarendon Press, 1965).

Jenkins, Harold D., "Some Aspects of the Background of *Rasselas*", in *Studies in English in Honor of Raphael Dorman O'Leary and Selden Lincoln Whitcomb* (Lawrence, Kansas, University of Kansas, 1940).

Joost, Nicholas, "Whispers of Fancy; or, the Meaning of *Rasselas*", *Modern Age*, I (Fall, 1957), 166—173.

Keast, William R., "Johnson's Criticism of the Metaphysical Poets", in *Eighteenth-Century English Literature: Modern Essays in Criticism*, edited by James L. Clifford (New York, Oxford University Press, 1959).

Kolb, Gwin J., "The Structure of *Rasselas*", *PMLA*, LXVI (September, 1951), 698—717.

—, "The 'Paradise' In Abyssinia and The 'Happy Valley' In Rasselas", *Modern Philology*, LVI (August, 1958), 10—16.

—, "Textual Cruxes in Rasselas", in *Johnsonian Studies*, edited by Magdi Wahba (Cairo, 1962).

Lascelles, Mary, "Rasselas Reconsidered", in *Essays and Studies 1951*, edited by Geoffrey Tillotson (London, John Murray).

Leyburn, Ellen Douglass, "No Romantick Absurdities or Incredible Fictions': The Relation of Johnson's *Rasselas* to Lobo's *Voyage to Abyssinia*", *PMLA*, LXXX (December, 1955), 1059—1067.

—, "Two Allegorical Treatments of Man: 'Rasselas' and 'La Peste' ", *Criticism 4* (Summer, 1962), 197—209.

Lockhart, Donald M., " The Fourth Son of the Mighty Emperor': The Ethiopian Background of Johnson's *Rasselas*", *PMLA*, LXXVIII (December, 1963), 516—528.

Lombardo, Agostino, "The Importance of Imlac", in *Bicentenary Essays on Rasselas*, edited by Magdi Wahba (Cairo Studies in English, 1959).

Mack, Maynard, Introduction to *The Augustans* (2nd ed., Englewood Cliffs, N. J., Prentice-Hall, Inc., 1961).

San Juan, E. Jr., "The Actual and the Ideal in Johnson's *Dictionary*", *University of Toronto Quartely*, XXXIV (January, 1965), 146—157.

Sherburn, George, "Rasselas Returns – To What?" *Philological Quarterly*, XXXVIII (July, 1959), 383—384.

Tracy, C. R. "Democritus, Arise!: A Study of Dr. Johnson's Humor", *Yale Review*, XXXIX (December 1949), 294—310.

Wasserman, Earl R., "The Inherent Values of Eighteenth-Century Personification", *PMLA*, LXV (June, 1950), 435—463.

Whitley, Alvin, "The Comedy of *Rasselas*", *ELH*, XXIII (March, 1956), 48—70.

Wimsatt, William K., Jr., "The Structure of the 'Concrete Universal' in Literature", *PMLA*, XLII (March, 1947), 262—280.

—, Introduction to *Selected Poetry and Prose* by Alexander Pope (New York, Rinehart & Co., 1951).

INDEX

Addison, Joseph, 10, 42, 45, 46, 47n, 48; *Guardian*, 40; "Vision of Mirzah", 57; *Tatler*, 63
Aeschylus, *Prometheus Bound*, 38—39, 42
Alice in Wonderland, 48
Allegory, 27—32 *esp.*; mentioned *passim*. *See also* allegorical metaphor *and* allegorical pun
Allegorical metaphor, 29—30, 32, 45, 51—52, 84, 92
Allegorical pun, 12, 45, 74, 80
Alvares, Francisco, 86
Aristotle, 28, 29

Bate, Walter Jackson, 19, 20, 22
Bloom, Edward, 81—82
Boswell, James 48n, 56, 84; *Life of Johnson*, 9, 10, 45
Boyce, Benjamin, 82
Bronson, Bertrand, 11, 18, 30, 31, 39, 44, 66
Bunyan, John, 10
Burke, Edmund, 48n
Burrowes, Rev. Robert, 13—14, 49

Carter, Mrs. Elizabeth, 79n
Cebes, *Table*, 40n, 62—64
Chapin, Chester F., 44
Choice of Hercules, 40n
Christie, O. F., 9, 66—67
Clifford, James L., 10, 89n
Coleridge, Samuel Taylor, 29
Collins, William, 44
Conant, Martha p., 87—88, 88n
Cowley, Abraham, 23, 37; "The Heartbreaking", 35

Daily Advertiser, 10
Dante, 32
Dennis, John, 43
de Urreta, Luis, 86

Dodsley, Robert, *Preceptor*, 56, 62—63
Donne, John, *First Anniversary*, 57n
Dryden, John, 47n, 50, 54; *Absalom and Achitophel*, 32n, 38, 83

Ebeling, Harry Alan, 10n, 79n
ecphrasis, 64
Empson, William, 45—46, 47n
Epictetus, *Manual*, 63
Euripides, *Alcestis*, 39, 42

Fielding, Henry, 72
Fletcher, Angus, 27n, 76
Ford, Samuel, 63
Frost, Robert, 29

Gray, Thomas, 44; "The Bard", 39
Greene, Donald J., 11, 97—98

Hagstrum, Jean H., 19—20, 21
Happy Valley, 12, 60, 75, 83—96
Healey, John, 63
Heinle, Edwin C., 40n, 56—57, 64n, 79—80
Huck Finn, 34
Hughes, John, 40—43

Imlac, 14, 17, 19n, 20—21, 59, 84, 88, 90, 94, 95

Jackson, W. T. H., 82
Jenkins, Harold D., 84—85
Johnson, Samuel, *Adventurer*, 23; *Dictionary*, 28, 37, 43, 48n, 50, 52, 53, 54, 56, 78, 80; *The Fountains*, 79, 80—81; *Idler*, 16, 22, 35, 79, 89; *Idler No. 22*, 76—79; Letter to the Earl of Chesterfield, 73; *Life of Addison*, 36; *Life of Cowley*, 35; *Life of Dryden*, 24—25, 36; *Life of Milton*, 38, 41—42; *Life of Pope,*

17, 36, 38, 61; *Life of Savage*, 17, 56; "London", 46*n*, 56; *Notes to Shakespeare*, 34*n*; "On the Death of Dr. Robert Levet", 39; *Preface to Shakespeare*, 21—22; *Preface to the English Dictionary*, 27; *Rambler*, 9, 10, 12, 15, 16, 21, 24, 26, 27, 50, 53, 54, 55, 56, 58, *esp.* 65—75, 79, 81, 92; *Rasselas*, 12, 14, 56, 59, 60, 70, 71, 75, *esp.* 83—96, 97. *(See also* Imlac *and* Happy Valley); "Vanity of Human Wishes", 46*n*, 56; "Vision of Theodore", 10, 12, *esp.* 56—64, 70—71

Jonson, Ben, 37
Joost, Nicholas, 87—92

Keast, William, R., 19—20
Keats, John, 98
King, Edward, 37
Kolb, Gwin, 85
Krutch, Joseph Wood, 96

Late Travels of S. Giacomo Baratti, 86
Le Grand, Abbé Joachim, 84—85
Lewis, C. S., 28, 29, 31—32
Leyburn, Ellen Douglass, 32*n*, 51, 54, 76—78, 82, 85
Lobo, Father Jerome, 84—85, 86
Lockhart, Donald, 85—86
Lombardo, Agostino, 94
Looker-On, 10

MacLeish, Archibald, 29
Mack, Maynard, 72
Mann, Thomas, 13*n*
Metaphor, 28—29, 34, 35, 37, 44, 48, 53, 55, 70, 71, 97, 98; dead metaphor, 49—52, 58, 80
Metaphysical poets, 36, 48
Milton, John, "Lycidas", 37; *Paradise Lost*, 57*n*, 86, 87
Mock-allegoric, 72—73
Mock-heroic, 72
Myth, 28

Obidah, 70
Ortogrul of Basra, 79—80

Parody, 32*n*
Pastoral, 77
Percy, Dr. Thomas, 10, 56

Personification, 29—30, 38—43, 66, 82
Personified Abstraction. *See* Personification
Pickrel, Paul, 32*n*
Plato, 63
Pope, Alexander, 47, 47*n*, 48—49, 68, 72; *Temple of Fame*, 41
Pun, 45—52, 53, 54, 55, 58. *See also* allegorical pun
Richards, I. A., 30*n*

Rowe, Nicholas, 22
Rymer, Thomas, 43

Satire, 55, 60*n*; allegorical satire, 76—77
Sawyer, Tom, 34
Shaftesbury, Earl of, 50, 51
Shakespeare, William, 15, 18, 21—22, 23, 43, 51, 98; *A Midsummer Night's Dream*, 34; *King Lear*, 50; *Titus Andronicus*, 50; Sonnet 138 (When my love swears that she is made of truth), 48
Shenstone, William, 10, 56
Sherburn, George, 94
Simile, 28, 35, 36, 37, 44
Socrates, 63
Spence, Joseph, 63*n*
Spenser, Edmund, 10, 54*n*, 63, 68
Stephen, Sir Leslie, 9
Swift, Jonathan, *Tale of a Tub*, 31; *Battle of the Books*, 60*n*
Symbol, 28, 30, 31

Tate, Allen, 31
Tenor and vehicle, 30*n*, 35, 37, 52, 80, 84, 98
Theobald, Lewis, 68
Theophrastan Character, 63, 68, 81—82
Tindall, William York, 28, 30
Twain, Mark, *Tom Sawyer Abroad* 34

Vehicle. *See* tenor and vehicle
Voltaire, 43; *Candide*, 88, 88*n*, 89

Williams, Anna, 80
Wimsatt, William K., 47—48, 49, 97
Whitley, Alvin, 91*n*